From Digital Traces to Algorithmic Projections

Cybersecurity Set

coordinated by
Daniel Ventre

From Digital Traces to Algorithmic Projections

Thierry Berthier
Bruno Teboul

First published 2018 in Great Britain and the United States by ISTE Press Ltd and Elsevier Ltd

ISTE Press Ltd
27-37 St George's Road
London SW19 4EU
UK

www.iste.co.uk

Elsevier Ltd
The Boulevard, Langford Lane
Kidlington, Oxford, OX5 1GB
UK

www.elsevier.com

For information on all our publications visit our website at http://store.elsevier.com/

British Library Cataloguing-in-Publication Data
A CIP record for this book is available from the British Library
Library of Congress Cataloging in Publication Data
A catalog record for this book is available from the Library of Congress
ISBN 978-1-78548-270-0

Printed and bound in the UK and US

Contents

Acknowledgements.   ix

Preface   xiii

Introduction   xv

Chapter 1. From the Philosophy of Trace to
Digital Traces   1

   1.1. Trace as a *"vestige"* and an *"imprint"*   1
   1.2. Trace and imprint with the value of an index and sign   5
   1.3. Trace for Heidegger, Levinas and Derrida   11
   1.4. Critical analysis of the concept of "digital trace"   16

Chapter 2. Formalism Associated with Algorithmic
Projections   23

   2.1. Projective formalism   24
      2.1.1. An operator's algorithmic S-projection   31
      2.1.2. An individual's global algorithmic projection   33
      2.1.3. Big data and bases for algorithmic projection   35
      2.1.4. Some examples of algorithmic projections.   36
      2.1.5. The volumes of an algorithmic projection   38
   2.2. E-reputation and algorithmic projections   39
      2.2.1. Digital reputation   39
      2.2.2. Brief history of e-reputation.   39
      2.2.3. An operator's systemic approach to e-reputation   41
   2.3. Competition, hacking and algorithmic projections.   43
      2.3.1. Competition, duels and algorithmic projections   43

2.4. The stakes for a projective data approach   44
2.4.1. Structuring massive data using the projective formalism   44

**Chapter 3. Connected Objects, a Location's Ubiquity
Level and the User's Algorithmic Consent**   49

3.1. The exponential evolution of connected objects
for 2020.   50
3.2. Projective formalism applied to connected objects.   53
3.3. A location's ubiquity level   55
3.4. An individual's algorithmic consent   56
3.5. The ubiquitous city, the generator of algorithmic projections   58
3.5.1. The example of U-Songdo, the first ubiquitous city   60
3.5.2. U-Songdo, ubiquitous city, or city of the future?   62
3.5.3. Predictive algorithms and feedback loops   63
3.5.4. The systemic loop "data-predictive-action"   64
3.5.5. The limits of predictive algorithms faced with
sheer chance.   65

**Chapter 4. On the Value of Data and Algorithmic
Projection.**   67

4.1. The complex problem of retrieving data.   67
4.2. How to define data value? The impact value
and instantaneous value of interpreting data   68
4.2.1. An influx of data to develop   68
4.2.2. Instantaneous value of data interpretation, impact
value and sale value   69
4.2.3. Instantaneous value of interpreting data   72
4.3. The value of a body of big data   79
4.3.1. The qualities of a body of big data in 6V   80
4.3.2. Value of a big data corpus.   81

**Chapter 5. False Data and Fictitious Algorithmic
Projections.**   85

5.1. Proliferation of fictitious data and fake profiles   85
5.1.1. An influx of false data and bots as the majority
of visitors   85
5.1.2. False data for protecting anonymity   87
5.1.3. Toward proliferation of fictitious profiles
on social networks   87
5.1.4. Purchasing fake subscribers to build popularity   89
5.1.5. The specific case of Twitter.   92

5.1.6. The Tinder networking application and
its derivatives   97
5.1.7. The "Robin Sage" experiment   98
5.2. Projective representation of fictitious data   100
5.2.1. The context of identity theft and the imitation
of a real individual   101
5.2.2. Context for the creation of fictitious profiles.   102
5.3. Fictitious algorithmic projections and cybersecurity.   105
5.3.1. Economic interference from fake profiles   105
5.3.2. A cyber-attack targeting a large consulting firm
from a fictitious profile   107
5.3.3. Attractive fictitious profiles (AFPs) in times of war   108
5.3.4. An influence operation by AFPs against
American soldiers, attributed to Russia.   110
5.3.5. China, Sun Tzu and AFPs   111

**Chapter 6. High-impact Cyber-operations Built
on Fictitious Algorithmic Projections**   113

6.1. The Newscaster cyber-espionage operation – NewsOnLine   113
6.1.1. A sophisticated operation   113
6.1.2. Modus operandi.   114
6.1.3. Confidence that arises from time and coherence   117
6.2. Attacks by HoaxCrash and false transfer orders:
the power of the cognitive lure   118
6.2.1. The human factor and cognitive lure: the keys to
HoaxCrash and false transfer order attacks   118
6.2.2. Attacks using HoaxCrash   119
6.2.3. False transfer order and BEC attacks   129
6.2.4. Automatic detection of attacks by HoaxCrash
and false transfer orders.   135

**Chapter 7. Prospective Epilogue: Global Algorithmic
Projection and NBIC Convergence**   139

7.1. A word on entropy.   139
7.2. Technology convergences and the spread of artificial
intelligence to domains of human expertise   140
7.3. NBIC convergence   140
7.4. CKTS   142

7.5. Convergence M-I (Material-Information) 143

7.6. The spread of artificial intelligence to domains
of human expertise 144

7.7. Global algorithmic projection and technology
convergences 146

Appendix 149

Bibliography 151

Index 161

Acknowledgements

Thierry Berthier

There is always an initial interaction or meeting, or conversation, that matures and gives rise to any book. This initiative came from Daniel Ventre, the series editor of ISTE's *Cybersecurity* series. Nearly 2 years ago, Daniel suggested, in his capacity as Saint-Cyr Chair in cyber defense and cybersecurity, that I collect numerous pieces of research on the concept of algorithmic projection to form a coherent work. My first thanks therefore go to him.

Next, I thank my friend Bruno Teboul, who took on the challenge of co-editing and exploring traces in philosophy and digital traces introducing the concept of projection. As the language of the philosopher is not always the language of the mathematician, Bruno has spared no effort in developing a philosophy of traces that remains accessible to non-specialists.

Finally, I thank my wife Marie-France for the long hours of reading and corrections, and my children, Antoine and Eloïse, for the stimulating discussions that pushed the work forward.

Bruno Teboul

To my children: Eve-Anaïs, Ysilde, Solal and Matthéo

I would like to thank in particular the *Université Technologique de Compiègne* and the team members at the Costech Laboratory to which I have belonged since September 2017 as associate researcher in the

Complexities, Networks and Innovation (CNI) team. The background and cross-disciplinary teams were really stimulating in hatching this excellent publication project.

To my teachers: Antonia Soulez, Monique Dixsaut, Michel Haar, Jean Largeault and Paul Mengal, who introduced me to philosophy, logic and epistemology at the *Université Paris Est* (Créteil Val de Marne).

This book is the result of my collaboration and friendship with Thierry Berthier since 2014, the year we first met.

I was working in the Keyrus group and I had just created the Data Scientist Chair at the *École Polytechnique*. At the same time, I was writing my doctoral thesis, which was an application of Actor Network Theory in the field of digital humanities. I was therefore interested in the problem and analysis of digital traces.

I developed, among other things the concept of "tracometry" in order to analyze scientific and profane digital traces on a specific and controversial subject: neuromarketing, while still taking an interest in work focusing on algorithmic projections. During this time, I considered the conceptual vacuum that dominated the subject of digital traces and together, we saw the opportunity to tackle the subject some months later.

We then started to co-write articles and organize conferences before deciding to co-edit a book that could return, from philosophical reflection on the concept of traces, to the analysis of digital traces, to carry out our research on algorithmic projections and their logical and mathematical formalization.

We share the same enthusiasm for bringing together science and technology and we are both convinced that exchanges and interactions between philosophy, logic and math are beneficial to the reflection on paths that are still uncertain and poorly signposted. The disciplines are complementary and there is no lack of examples of books or authors on the boundaries of both fields: from Descartes, Leibniz, Kant, Husserl, Russell, Whitehead, Carnap, to all the members of the "Vienna Circle", Turing, Von Neumann, Hilbert and so on.

The path opening from the intersection of philosophy and mathematical logic enables the formalism to form new knowledge, to build new reasoning and to avoid contradictions and paradoxes around tricky and sometimes confusing concepts. We judge that our modest contribution in the thread of this great tradition, put forward in this work, may partake in this Leibnizian or Hilbertian optimism.

Preface

The Calumny of Apelles – Sandro Botticelli, 1475 (source:
The Yorck Project, 10,000 Meisterwerke der Malerei,
DIRECTMEDIA Publishing GmbH, 2002)

The Calumny of Apelles is one of the master Sandro Botticelli's major works. Painted in 1495, it depicts 10 minor goddesses from Greek mythology. Hera, the deceived goddess, learns that the deified heroine Semele is pregnant with Dionysus by Zeus. Furious about this new infidelity, Hera goes to look for Apate, the goddess of deception. She hopes in this way to prevent Semele from becoming the new queen of the heavens in her place. To keep her position, Hera asks Apate to lend her the belt of deception, which will bring back her husband and son. Whoever wears this belt can make the person they desire do anything they wish. Apate obeys Hera and so opens Pandora's box, the source of a thousand ills and deceptions that spread over the earth.

On the right of Botticelli's painting are the minor goddesses: Apate (deception), Agnoia (ignorance), Diabole (calumny), Epiboule (astuteness), Hypolepsis (distrust), Metanoia (regret) and Pteropode (envy). On the left of the painting, Aletheia, the goddess of truth, raises her right hand against the rising threats.

For over more than five centuries, this extraordinary work has represented to perfection the major goddesses of cybersecurity who operate in a cyberspace ever more prey to digital attacks and deception. Greek mythology has not ceased to surprise us with its modernity and its capacity to project mankind's passions onto the gods. Two millennia later, the projection of human competition, conflicts, duels and weaknesses has left the realm of mythology for the digital realm, but its minor goddesses are still there, maneuvering just behind our keyboards and our screens.

Thierry BERTHIER
Bruno TEBOUL
June 2018

Introduction

The 20th Century saw the acceleration of technical progress with innovations that transformed our environment and influenced our actions. The digital revolution, which should objectively be called the "Turing era", began in the 1930s with the founding work of Alan Turing (1912–1954), the father of modern information technology, calculability, Turing machines and the halting problem. At the same time, the research of Andrei Kolmogorov (1903–1987) on algorithmic information theory and complexity enabled the discovery of new territories in the domain of calculation. Modern IT bears the DNA of the giants Turing and Kolmogorov. Our interactions with electronic machines, small or large, connected or unconnected, are the leaves of a tree planted by Turing and Kolmogorov. We are indebted to them when we use our email or buy something on the Internet. Our digital deeds and actions carry their traces. Of course, they are not the only contributors to the rise of IT in the last seven decades, but their contributions were decisive in the arrival of a functioning cyberspace.

Today, almost all of us have a more or less hectic "digital life", which happens during working hours, and during periods of leisure and relaxation. Our daily habits with electronic systems and our voluntary or involuntary interactions with machines produce ever more substantial volumes of data. These digital traces say a great deal about our habits, our tastes and our choices. They are now a faithful reflection of our activities. In terms of information, this digital reflection focuses part of our projected image according to algorithms carried out on machines.

The concept of digital traces

A digital trace can be defined as a set of binary words (words of finite length formed of 0 and 1) forming a file created and archived on a system after a voluntary or forced interaction between a human user and this system. The digital trace is born with the capacity to store a datum over the long term on a magnetic or electronic support. Running a program on a system with calculation capabilities often requires input data to initialize the calculation and provide the output result (output data). During the calculation, "collateral" data or metadata can be created *and* stored. Output data and collateral data stored on the system form the digital trace created from the "man–system" interaction (Figure I.1).

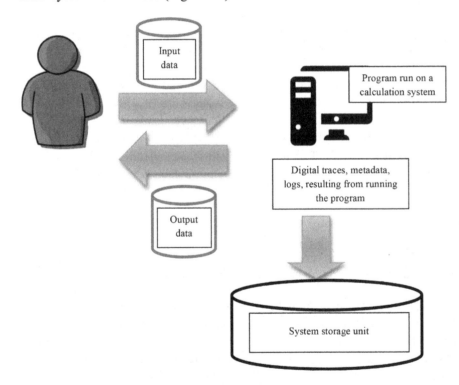

Figure I.1. *Mechanism for creating digital traces*

In practice, there are few "man–system" interactions that do not produce a digital trace. A day of activity in the life of an ordinary citizen in a technologically developed country is in effect a day spent producing digital traces. Using a cellphone creates traces that make it possible to geolocate and identify the user with very high probability. Four antenna traces are sufficient to identify them with more than 95% certainty. On a highway with tolls, passing through a toll booth and payment using an automatically recognized badge produces digital traces that make it possible to precisely track the journey and hours of movement. In the same way, using a railcard during train or bus journeys causes digital traces to be created that archive the details of movement. In business, pointing operations using electronic badges produce traces that reveal the employee's presence at their workplace. At a supermarket, radio-frequency chips are replacing barcodes on products. They are important vectors for digital traces that, once used, reveal the consumer's choices, preferences and buying habits. It is then possible to characterize an individual by their shopping basket and by the place and time of the transaction. The healthcare sector is an important source of digital traces. In France, the setting up of a personal medical file (PMF) makes it possible to follow the patient and their illnesses better by recording each medical step and examination taken. Even in anonymous form, digital traces linked to the PMF say a great deal about our health practices. Air transport is endowed with a broad range of digital tools dedicated to flight security. The PNR (Passenger Name Record) is formed of the personal data of all the passengers onboard a single airplane. It allows optimal traceability before boarding and forms part of a counter-terrorism policy. The resulting digital traces make it possible to establish traveler profiles and are involved in calculating the risk linked to a given profile. On the Internet, online commerce relies on an ever more refined knowledge of the consumer, their behavior and preferences. Personalized marketing uses traces from commercial transactions. The connected objects all generate traces produced by their sensors. Video surveillance systems endowed with facial recognition capabilities complete the construction of digital identity using images.

The growing set of an individual's digital traces gathers voluntary traces resulting from interactions decided by the user and involuntary traces produced during automatic interactions with a system. Voluntary traces may come from messages, photos and videos posted on a blog or on social networks, data published on an online CV, reviews left on online shopping sites and data inserted into forms or profiles completed on a forum. Involuntary traces are created during a visit to a website. The IP address, operating system and the last pages visited by the user can appear in the form of traces. Requests and key words entered into a search engine are recorded and produce significant traces. Cookies (short files placed on the machine of a visitor to a website) are vectors of traces. The total of all digital traces, voluntary or not, produced by an individual, forms their digital identity. Nevertheless, a trace only has meaning when it is associated with a context and this is not always known or accessible.

Digital identity

A user's digital identity is formed from various sources: personal data associated with their different profiles, information that they publish on the Web, information that others publish about them and the traces that they leave, consciously or not, on specialist platforms.

Digital identity aggregates entities that consist of opinion (what I like or dislike), knowledge (what I know), expertise (my profession, my experience), representation (my appearance), location (how and where to meet me), reputation (what is being said about me), expression (what I say), publication (what I share), purchases (what I buy) and audience (who I know). Linking and crossing these different entities often makes it possible to find out new information on the "traced" individual. The great significance of the set of traces is often under-estimated by the user – a producer who only has a local perception of their digital footprint.

The perimeter of an individual's digital identity varies greatly depending on their psychology.

The researcher, Dominique Cardon (*Le design de la visibilité*; an essay on web typology 2.0 – 2018), has put forward a typology of forms of online presence by describing five visibility formats organized on the pairing: digital identity/type of sought visibility:

Format 1 – "The screen": this means "to hide, to be seen" and shows itself for example by frequenting meet-up sites.

Format 2 – "The light-dark": this means "to show oneself as hidden". Participants make all or part of their personal and daily lives visible to a social network of acquaintances.

Format 3 – "The beacon": this means "to show all, to see all" while searching for maximal connectivity.

Format 4 – "The magic lantern": this means "seen but hidden" and uses avatars to separate real and virtual identity.

Format 5 – "The post-it" meaning "I'm there, I'm doing this". Participants make their availability and presence visible to all but only interact with a restricted circle.

According to Dominique Cardon, this typology makes it possible to define four main classes of digital identity: civil identity, acting identity, narrative identity and virtual identity.

Civil identity is associated with the "screen" format. It is built by using platforms such as Twitter, Facebook and Meetic. Linked to the "self" and to real life, it refers to the individual's education, profession, location, availability, matrimonial status, physical characteristics and moods.

Acting identity is linked to the "beacon" format. It results from the use of platforms such as LinkedIn, Wikipedia or Flickr. It reflects the context of activities, social engagements, hobbies, passions and communities of interest. It belongs to the categories "reality" and "activity".

Narrative identity is linked to the "light-dark" format and results from the use of platforms such as Skyblog or LiveJournal. It reflects the "hidden self" – introspection, descriptions of daily life, and a personal or literary diary. It belongs to the categories "self" and "projection".

Virtual identity is linked to the "magic lantern" format and results from the use of platforms such as YouTube, MySpace, Second Life or World of Warcraft. It is built on borrowed personas, online gaming profiles, avatars, self-produced content, audience meters and scripts. It belongs both to the categories "activity" and "projection".

Seen as the sum of the digital traces relating to an individual or group, digital identity is formed of heterogonous data, which is more or less durable over time. The platforms that have generated traces may have disappeared by the time the data is observed. Traceability of digital identity is therefore never totally assured without access to a complete history of all the examined profile's digital interactions.

The limits of the concept of the digital trace

The digital trace is limited to a finite set of binary words stored on an archiving unit on a calculation system. The trace as such "says" nothing about its origin: who was it created by? What algorithm implemented it? How? Voluntarily or as a simple system interaction?

The lack of information mounted on the trace makes it difficult to formulate. Attributing a trace to a source (recovery) often requires additional data that do not figure in the trace considered. If the concept of trace suffices in an unstructured description of digital identity, then it proves insufficient when it comes to characterizing or categorizing it more finely.

The uncertainties limiting the concept of trace provoke the following questions:

– How can we identify the system on which the trace was initially produced?

– Which algorithm implemented or run on this system produced this trace?

– What individual is at the root of the trace?

– How can we authenticate a trace's origin?

– To what digital identity should it be linked?

The contributions of projective formalism

In its formalism, the projective representation of a trace answers these questions and makes it possible to characterize an individual's digital identity depending on the algorithms implemented and the systems on which they have been run, voluntarily or not, by an individual. The concept of algorithmic projection enriches that of trace by giving it, declaratively, its origin and algorithmic structure. It makes it possible to describe the set of traces formally using an ascending approach (bottom-up) starting from the finest rung: an individual's algorithmic projection on a system S according to an algorithm A run on this at a given instant. Joining the basic algorithmic projections created on a single system S by an individual then gives rise to their S-projection. Finally, joining all the individual's S-projections creates their global algorithmic projection, a witness to their digital identity.

If the projective approach facilitates the categorization of digital traces, the formalism of algorithmic projections makes it possible to define new invariants such as a place's ubiquity level and an individual's algorithmic consent.

In cybersecurity and cyber defense segments, algorithmic projections are naturally involved in the complex problem of retrieving a digital datum: how and by whom was this datum produced? On what system and according to which algorithm?

Finally, the projective representation makes it possible to formalize the creation of fictitious data architectures (FDA) that often form the input and initialization vector for sophisticated cyber-attacks. Digital identity theft and the creation of false profiles on social networks allow a projective description.

The itinerary chosen for exploring the concept of projection

Our study suggests a projective approach to digital traces relying on a formalism including the individual, the system and the algorithm run. The broad concept of trace is explored from a philosophical angle in Chapter 1. We show that it is not sufficient to describe the exchanges of information at the root of the formation of digital traces. It should be replaced by a concept of projection that involves all the trace's actors: the human user, the system and the algorithm.

The complete formalism describing algorithmic projections is explained in Chapter 2. This is still, however, accessible to readers who are not specialists in mathematics.

Focusing on connected objects, Chapter 3 presents two unpublished concepts: a place's level of ubiquity and an individual's algorithmic consent.

Chapter 4 queries the value of data. How should it be described? How is it formed according to the body of data?

False data, the initial vectors of digital insecurity and the matrices of cybercrime, are studied from the angle of projection in Chapter 5 by emphasizing, in particular, the powerful mechanisms operating on social networks.

Focusing on fictitious data structures, Chapter 6 concentrates on the high-impact cyber-attacks created from fictitious algorithmic projections.

Chapter 7 appears as a prospective epilogue analyzing the likely development of our global algorithmic projection under the effect of the convergence of NBIC (Nanotechnologies, Biotechnologies, IT, Cognitive science) technologies.

Readers with backgrounds that are literary rather than scientific are invited to take the time necessary to read passages containing the mathematic formalism, and to not "skip over" them because they are written with this in mind and do not require any mathematical background.

1

From the Philosophy of
Trace to Digital Traces

1.1. Trace as a *"vestige"* and an *"imprint"*

The concept of trace is both a subject of research for numerous disciplines and an open and complex question. However, what is a trace for a philosopher, an archaeologist, an historian, a psychologist, a criminologist, an IT technician or a mathematician? How does the concept of trace make it possible to find points of semantic, philological and methodological convergence or divergence, between its disciplines? According to what processes are traces made visible for these disciplines in general? What definition of trace can we suggest? Is a philosophy of trace possible? What main, contemporary philosophical movements have considered trace?

To try to provide at least part of an answer to these many research questions, we suggest envisaging the concept of trace according to three axes for consideration that will borrow from contemporary philosophy: we will start by trying to produce a general definition of the concept of *"trace"*, and then we will envisage it as a *"vestige"*, an *"imprint"*, a *"spectrum"* and a *"sign"*, to discuss, finally, the Heideggerian, Levinassian and Derridian views of trace and its importance in relation to contemporary philosophy.

In fact, before asking questions on *"digital traces"*, it first makes sense to critically query the concept of "trace". In this book, we will specify the possible definition of the term "digital" contained in the phrase "digital trace", to understand its significance and to discuss its semantic constituent and association. It can already be said that it is thanks to the *"growing role played in IT environments that digital traces have been the trigger for reflection to further the notion of trace. If the term seems self-evident in the context of IT, the question of its definition is nevertheless quickly asked. What are the particle properties of these digital data that explain why they are called traces? If these digital traces are really kinds of traces, we need to understand better what traces are when the word is used in other contexts*" [MIL 13].

Therefore, we start by recalling the etymological origin of the concept of "trace". A philological approach to the concept of "trace" will enable us to understand its polysemy better, to envisage the articulation of a complex and transdisciplinary thought. Trace resonates as a central theme in many research domains, as mentioned above, and reasons using tools and methods from subjects as diverse as history, archaeology, psychology, philosophy, mathematics, IT or indeed criminology.

Etymologically, the word "vestige" comes from the Latin word "*vestigium*" which means "trace" in English. As the Collins dictionary states, it is "a footprint or other indication of the passage of an animal or person" [COL 14]. If we go back to Old High German and the German language, we will note, for example, that trace is translated as the term "*Spur*" which itself also comes from "*vestigium*" and originally meant "the imprint of a foot". According to the history of the term, "*Spüren*" ("*to perceive*"), i.e. the act of finding and following a path, is intimately linked to this meaning. Sybille Krämer tells us, in an article from 2012:

"The subject (trace) and activity (perceiving) enter into an elementary relationship, not however because this activity relates to the act of producing traces – as will become evident, but rather to the act of interpreting and following them. It is not therefore the formation of a trace, but rather the use made of it after it is created that is clearly the form of activity 'corresponding' to the trace. Is it therefore established that only the use that is made of a trace makes such? The usual meaning of 'trace', as 'a series of footprints or impressions left on the ground by someone or something passing' is not the only one to look back to the primitive idea of a footprint. Technical acceptances of this term also refer to the act of 'following a track': when 'Spur' ('path') refers to part of a magnetic band" [KRÄ 07].

Henceforth, we can ask ourselves the following questions to begin our analysis: *"is 'trace' a generic term, of which 'footprint' and 'vestige' are sub-species? Should any be thought of as a vestige, residue, remainder? Each of these terms assumes a different relationship with the past. But what? The case of 'vestige' is the simplest. Perhaps 'vestige' says all that remains to us of a lost past: the ruins of a castle, an archaeological site, a family heirloom, etc."* [GRE 03]. In fact, as Jean Greisch tells us, the trace defined as a *"vestigium"* immediately tells us the former time dimension of the process by which the trace is produced.

We see, we observe, we note, we identify a trace that is always there, marked with the seal of the past; any trace is a trace of the past, as it marks, shows and indicates a past event which is finished. This is how a direct link can be established between the production of a trace, and the imprint it leaves, which subsists in human and natural activities, which include the structures, objects and traces themselves left by the passage of man, which are most often reduced to the state of vestiges, following the degradations that occur over time.

"As an initial analysis, we believe that a trace is formed from footprints left voluntarily or not in the environment when a process occurs. The trace thus formed is inscribed (or not) in the environment used as a support for memory (as a process). The nature of footprints is very variable and any process can produce (or not) more or less persistent footprints, inscribed in the environment and then distinguishable by knowledgeable observers as a trace of the initial process. Observation is therefore a cognitive process for distinguishing (in the proper sense) the footprint as a trace of something that can make sense" [MIL 13].

A trace is made over time; it is over time that it forms as a trace and it is over the course of time that it appears as a footprint, an imprint in time, an imprint from a past time, from which it subsists, resists and persists in the present time. A trace resulting from the past shows itself to the present to perpetuate its imprint, its meaning: that is, its significance and direction.

If we compare this definition to the way in which archaeology uses the concept of trace, we see that, in archaeological lexicon, a trace is also considered to be a vestige, the vestige of a mark left by a human action resulting from mankind or nature, such as steps, frequent passage, the application of dye, the breakdown of organic matter in the soil or lines etched or painted on a stone wall. For archaeology, these vestiges act as paleontological, anthropological, historical, economic, social and cultural witnesses.

"The observer should therefore be warned (of the traced object) to distinguish, interpret and use traces that will adopt the status of inscriptions of knowledge in their cognitive context. We therefore suggest, arbitrarily and for ease at this stage, to call an imprint the inscription of something in the environment at the time of the process and trace the observation of this imprint in a time that cannot predate it (but may be the same). Some examples illustrating the imprint/trace distinction: fingerprints are left at the site of a crime and will be considered as traces by the enquirer who will identify them as such for their enquiry (a voluntary inscription of the trace); in a work of literature, forms of writing will amount to imprints considered as a trace by a knowing reader (a critic or amateur). Naturally, traces as developed in different disciplines break down into forms and for different objects, for example: for the tale of a historical epic, for the running or analysis of a melody, for monitoring the development of vegetables, for a scene in a film, for refining software, for studying the life of a cell, for carrying out a police inquest, for ensuring that personal data is remembered, for taking account of a mathematical demonstration, for facilitating a workshop with group of students, for following particle collisions, for monitoring the running of a program, for taking account of interactions in a social network, etc." [MIL 13].

The trace's *archaeology* (in the sense of discussing the basics) is based on the principle that an imprint becomes a trace when it is analyzed and interpreted as such. The imprint inscribed in a particular field of knowledge, a discipline (criminology, IT, etc.), gives the cognition that results from it a *"revealed"* character: the trace is the *"revealed"* manifestation and the *"unveiled"* result of this knowledge inscribed in the imprint. We can thus speak of a *phenomenology of trace* from reading and observing imprints.

1.2. Trace and imprint with the value of an index and sign

In contemporary philosophy and especially in phenomenology, we can also consider trace as an imprint with the value of an index or sign: *"in the eyes of a phenomenologist who is interested in the multiple modes in which phenomena are given, an imprint presents in no less complex a manner. The simplest case is that of the footprints of someone walking in the sand beside the sea or a goat's feet in the snow. Traces of this type show us that someone, man or animal, 'has been here'. They have a value that can be described as 'indicational', arising from this very general class of signs that Husserl calls in the first* Logical Investigations: *'Anzeichen', 'indices'. Perhaps we can add, in reference to the famous distinction between icon, index and symbol in Charles Sanders Peirce's semiotics, that unlike the icon (which refers to the designated object by virtue of its own character, independent of the question of knowing if this object really exists or not) and unlike the symbol (which refers to it by virtue of a law or rule), 'the index is a sign that refers to the object because it is really affected by the object'. This is evidently the case with the imprints that I have just mentioned"* [GRE 03].

Paul Ricoeur perceives in *Plato's Theaetetus* the first theoretical framework for this ancient problem, the essence of the trace as imprint. *"In this dialogue between Socrates and a sophist, Plato established a relationship between two problems: on the one hand, that of the eikon, i.e. the image, or the imagination, or even the 'present representation of something which is absent', on the other hand, that of the tupos, the imprint, approached by the metaphor of a block of wax, which it is useful to mention briefly. For Plato, the combination of these two problems frames the question of the truth and error, error being assimilated with the erasure of marks or misunderstanding, a failure to adapt the image to its imprint. What is this metaphor of the block of wax, which illustrates the problem of the imprint, the tupos, for Plato? It compares the soul (or the spirit) to a block of wax, which may be very different depending on the individual (smaller or larger, more or less malleable, etc.) and which serves to imprint, to engrave sensations or thoughts (semeia). These sensations or thoughts are recalled by memory and form knowledge, whereas what cannot be recalled has been forgotten, and 'we do not know it'"* [SER 02].

The "*block of wax metaphor*" is fundamental, as it is part of the intersection of a triple dialectic: between memory and forgetting, between knowledge and ignorance, between truth and error, since Plato defined truth or a true opinion as what comes from the memory's faithfulness to the imprint, whereas error or false opinion comes from lack of faithfulness to the imprint. For Ricoeur, Socrates thought that "*a false opinion resides not in the relations of perceptions to one another, or of thoughts to one another, but in the connecting (sunapsis) of perception of thought*" [RIC 00]. A direct relationship is thus placed between the imprint (*tupos*) and memory, as a "*block of wax*", formed of marks (*semeia*), which convey the "*affections of the body and the soul*", the imagination and the image (*eikon*) of these imprints, of these marks, which is the art of imitation, a simulacrum or similitude. Moreover, knotted into these three, still according to Ricoeur, is the problem of truth and the "*truthful dimension of memory and history*", as an adjustment and faithfulness to the imprint; this "*dialectic of accommodation, harmonization and adjustment between the eikon and the imprint is able to succeed or fail*" [GRE 03].

A dialectic is also observed between absence and presence forged within the same Ricoeurian concept of trace: why is the presence of the trace witness to the absence of what it has formed? This dialectic of presence and absence is found to be at the center of Ricoeur's philosophical concerns and his approach to trace, especially when he mentions the subject of death from the historian's point of view, which he opposes to the Heideggerian ontology of being-faced-with-death: "*an ontology of the being-faced-with-death, against-death, where the work of morning is taken into account. Heidegger's boundary established between the notions of vestige and trace becomes less water-tight if we give a 'more carnal touch' to existential historicity. A reflection on the Greek Lethe, inseparable from the Greek idea of Aletheia, as Heidegger does not cease to remind us, suggests that all memory has its sources in an initial lack of memory and an originating origin (Ursprung), distinct from a simple beginning. In this sense, we can speak of a 'founding forgetfulness', which makes historical memory itself possible. Far from being synonymous with destruction, forgetting then takes on a positive meaning. By drinking deeply from the 'waters of Lethe', mentioned in the final myth of the Republic, we discover that 'having-been makes forgetting the immemorial resource provided to the work of remembering'*" [GRE 03].

Trace can also be defined and understood as a spectrum in the sense that Roland Barthes uses the word; he believes that trace takes account of a *"spectral spectacle"*, a trace of something that is no longer there, but which has left its mark, as in photography, for example. We can therefore speak of trace as the ghost of a process that has taken place. *"In photography, the presence of the thing (at a certain, past moment) is never metaphorical and for living beings, it is not their life either, unless one is photographing dead bodies; and still: if the photography is consequently horrible, it is because it attests, if we can say so, that the corpse is living, as a corpse: it is the living image of a dead thing. The effect that it produces on me is not to reform what has been destroyed (by time and distance), but to attest that what I see really existed. I read at the same time, it will be and it has been; I observe with horror a future perfect whose death is a challenge. By giving me the pose's absolute past, photography tells me of death in the future. By attesting that the object was once real, it surreptitiously makes one think it is living, because of the temptation that makes us attribute an absolutely superior value to the real, as eternal; yet on transferring this reality to the past ('it has been'), it suggests it is already dead"* [BAR 80].

Trace in Barthes' sense is a ghost, in the sense that it is a living witness of what is not living, a present testimony of the past: passed, but giving the impression of always being present. The ghost of trace gives way to Barthes' spectral trace, which means the immortalization of the present moment as a lure which remains and can be grasped, while still not really being more present.

"In Camera Lucida, *such a distinction has evidently not been theorized and the challenge of the attempt lies on the contrary in an imperceptible confusion between past, present, and future perfect: from the certainty of 'this has been', that Barthes posits as the noeme of photography, to the future – foreshadowed but still nonetheless past: 'he is dead and he will die'. Subtly, the writer thus seems to play with photography's desire for a spectral presence, which would sometimes emphasize and sometimes undo the outrage of death. Photography, in fact, like any recording art, infinitely reproduces what has only happened once: it repeats mechanically what can never more be repeated existentially"* [ZEN 16].

The concept of *Barthes' ghost* is interesting here, too, to categorize digital traces, which in English are often linked especially to "*shadow data*" or "*phantom data*", or even "*spectral information*".

In one sense, we could say that there is both a memory of trace and an inscription of trace: "*the physical inscription of any trace*" which recalls Bruno Bachimont's *support theory* [MAR 16], which, in a cross-disciplinary field, extends from philosophical research to the cognitive sciences, has shown that "knowledge can only proceed from an inscription on a support material" [BAC 00]. This definition will also act as an anchor for the idea of digital trace in section 1.4.

Jean Griesch reminds us that the concept of "trace" leads us to two sources of confusion: the first asks the question of trace as an "index category", or even as a "sign" and the second would be more phenomenological, happily referring to Ricoeur, Husserl and then Parmenides, defining trace as a "*sign-effect*".

Ricoeur brings us face to face with this problem: "*so much as to appear, so much as to be*" *is just as valuable in phenomenology. The "phenomenon" is what appears in the field of consciousness. Indeed, "trace" refers us to what does not appear. This does not prevent effects from being produced, scarcely perceptible in some cases and very speculative in others. While still careful not to define the sign generally, Husserl develops a reflection on the two fundamental categories of signs with which we are dealing: simple indices* (Anzeichen) *and expressions endowed with meaning. The question I would like to raise in the context of this study, while bearing in mind that I do not have the means to answer it, is to know if it would be possible to produce, in the wake of Husserl's phenomenology, but in debate with the neurosciences and psychanalysis, a "logical" research, whose title would not be:* Ausdruck und Bedeutung *("expression and meaning"), but:* Spur und Deutung *("trace and interpretation"). Indeed, trace seems to us rather to be drawn from the side of* apousia *(absence), of* Abwesen *(absence). For some metaphysical thought, which can be recognized in the elderly Parmenides' command, trace appears as a dangerous deceiver: "but whatever is simultaneously absent as well as present, knows that it sees, through thought, with a look that nothing can turn away; since being will never disconnect from dependence on being any longer, thus it is dispersed in all directions and at the same time comes to form a whole*" [GRE 03].

"*A trace is not manufactured, it is left, and without any intention*" [KRÄ 07]. This phrase, coined by Sybille Krämer, assumes that the trace which we speak of here is a so-called "natural" trace, a trace that has not been manufactured, which is produced by nature or left by one of its creatures (animal or human) and the production of trace is termed "unintentional"; a natural trace is therefore produced without its authors being aware of it.

Trace always assumes an authenticity, an essential truth, that we could call ontic ("being") or indeed ontological (being from being) depending on the various understandings suggested by the phenomenology of trace. However, we will see that the question of authenticity, of the ontic and ontological truth of digital trace, as an "*artifactual trace*", creates a problem and is posed as one of the fundamental problems that contemporary philosophy must face and overcome when thinking of "*digital trace*".

This conceptual and theoretical breaking point is essential, as we will see when we distinguish the original concept of ("natural" or "anthropic") "trace" and its interpretation and use contained in the syntagm "digital trace"; since "digital traces", which can quite clearly be manufactured, erased, falsified, corrupted, etc., require that we understand the definition in the light of the concepts of the truth and authenticity of digital trace (these are points that we will discuss below, in section 1.4 of the present book).

We can decide at any moment to modify, alter or indeed delete a trace, whatever it is, but as Sybille Krämer rightly says: "*similarly, the act of erasing traces amounts to leaving one. And vice versa: as soon as a trace is knowingly left and staged as such, it is no longer a trace. Only that which is not intentional, which is involuntary, uncontrolled and arbitrary, etches or draws these lines of rupture that can be read as tracks. Unlike the sign, which we create, the meaning of a trace exists beyond the intention of whoever creates it. It is precisely whatever escapes our attention, our control or our vigilance that, through our acts, takes the form of a trace: it is not the consciousness but the 'weight' and materiality of the Being that forge traces*" [KRÄ 07].

The theories of Charles Sanders Peirce have suffered from too great a fragmentation to have a real and durable impact in Europe. However, Peirce's thought achieved a wealth that makes it indispensable to philosophy and semiotics [TIE 13].

The sign, according to Charles Sanders Peirce, is formed by the relationship of three components that can be moved closer to the triadic model (without however being able to assimilate them entirely), and that are called *representamen* or *sign* (for the signifier), *object* (for the referent) and *interpretant* (for the signified). *"A sign, or representamen, is something which takes the place of something for someone in some relationship or capacity. It is addressed to someone, i.e. it creates in this person's mind an equivalent or perhaps a more developed sign. This sign that it creates, I will call the first sign's interpretant. This sign takes the place of a thing: of its object. It takes the place of this object, not in all its relations, but by reference to a sort of idea that I have sometimes called the basis of the representamen"* [PEI 89].

Charles Sanders Peirce differentiates the immediate object, that is, a referent in the strict, fixed sense, without which the sign would not exist, but which does not cover all of the existing possibilities for the dynamic object, a broader referent, which includes what the sign cannot directly express but can only indicate, and which the receiver should interpret in light of their experience.

Charles Sanders Pierce distinguishes an immediate interpretant, that is, a probable meaning, likely to come to mind spontaneously from any receiver who knows the code, a dynamic interpretant, the particular meaning formed in the mind of a particular receiver at each instance of reception (which can result in an action), and a final interpretant, a meaning on which all of the receivers can agree, or, if we can say so, the "correct" or "authorized" meaning.

According to Charles Sanders Pierce, *"in the light of external facts, the only manifestations of thought that we might find are thoughts through signs. It is clear that the existence of any other thought cannot be proven through external facts. But we have seen that it is only through external facts that the thought can be known. The only thought, then, that is knowable for us, is thought through signs. But a thought that cannot be known does not exist. Any thought should therefore necessarily be thought through a sign"* [PEI 84].

This model includes some elements that are lacking in what we have seen above, and which make it possible to understand the process of *semiosis* in a pragmatic and communicative context. The distinction between the immediate and the dynamic makes it possible to separate what is recognized and decoded mechanically, and effective interpretation by a receiver, for example a word's definition(s) as written in a dictionary and the meaning of a word in context.

It is therefore clear that the sign has no immanence, but exists only because a semiosis has taken place in the mind of the interpreter (receiver). Moreover, this interpreter is not abstract or idealized, but reacts to the sign according to their personal experience (depending on a dynamic interpretant), while there is an "average" reaction sanctioned by culture, the final interpretant. Consequently, by "sign", we should understand both a signifying potentiality and a particular interpretative act.

1.3. Trace for Heidegger, Levinas and Derrida

"In the twentieth century, it was above all Heidegger, Levinas and Derrida who addressed the theme of trace from a new angle. More precisely, they addressed it in the context of a criticism and deconstruction of metaphysics: trace becomes the site of difference and otherness. Heidegger opposes the rational utilitarianism of technique with experience of the pretheoretical reality formed by poetry. For Levinas, the concept of trace refers to the limits of the interpretability or intelligibility of the Other, which cannot be interpreted precisely. It is not technological rationality that Levinas opposes when he brings trace to light as a characteristic trait of the Other, but the semiotic-hermeneutic grasping of the Other, it being understood that this grasping is subordinated to the egology of a self-mastering subject. As for Derrida, he correlates semiology and trace, maintaining that any sign becomes the trace of other signs through a difference that refers it at once to all the others and at the same time excludes it from these. Thus, trace forms the basis of our symbolic relationship with the world. Derrida calls this 'differance', naming by this term an incessant dynamic of returns and differentiations that prevents us from ever, by and in thought, going back to an origin or even a definitive conclusion" [KRÄ 07].

In his book *La mémoire, l'histoire, l'oubli,* Ricoeur [RIC 00] considers trace according to three distinct realities, which must not be confused: *"mnesic trace"*, which is cerebral or cortical; *"mnemonic trace"*, which is conscious or unconscious; finally, *"written trace"* which plays a central role in *"historiographic"* operation, but which also defines writing in its more general sense, what Derrida calls *"archi-writing"* or *"architrace"*.

Derrida defines the concept of *"archi-trace"* from phenomenology and linguistics. The phonic substance must be neutralized, as it is the difference that gives shape to the sound, and not the other way round. So that there is a difference, there must first be a retention of an original trace, of an imprint: nothing other than the trace, which does not exist in the present but imprints a movement where writing and speech are articulated. This movement is the *condition* of any inscription, whether it is phonic or graphic; it grounds classic opposites: sensible/intelligible, signifying/signified, expression/content.

Remember that, in *"differance"*, [DER 72a] Derrida offers a series of writings of trace leading to the *heideggerian frühe Spur* of the ontological difference. Martin Heidegger tells us in *La parole d'Anaximandre* [HEI 87] that the original trace of ontological difference, which has been erased and forgotten, leaves only a secondary trace of its erasure in language texture; this original trace is nevertheless always imagined in terms of primitive experience. Heidegger always maintains that trace, which we can experience in language, amounts to an erased trace, which was already a present experience for the first Greek philosophers.

Jacques Derrida relied on Peirce's definition of *semiosis ad infinitum,* which we explained above to develop the two notions of the deconstruction of meaning and the interpretative drift that surpasses any restriction.

When he was developing his concept of trace in the 1960s, Derrida wanted it to be *unlimited*. It cannot be reduced to an inscription on a support or to writing (simple material inscription). Any experience in life, whether it is human or animal, is a reference to the other, a difference in movement, a differance. It leaves a wake that can be retained, kept and archived, but which can also be lost; as the loss of a trace is not circumstantial, it is structural. A trace can always be erased, be forgotten and disappear.

This is especially the characteristic of digital traces in the era of the web and cognitive and quantum IT, and all electronic files in general. In addition, Derrida introduced this in 1967 in a major text *"De la grammatologie"* [DER 67], where he brings together what he calls *"electronic files and reading machines"* (the precursors of computers) of his concepts of trace and grammè, and which will enable us to analyze *"digital traces"* in section 1.4.

What Jacques Derrida calls *"grammatology"* is not a *"human science"* among others, as the question it asks, his question, is what the name of mankind is. Most human groups designate themselves "man", and use the usual criteria (intelligence, speech, an organized society, etc.) to distinguish themselves; other living beings do not escape *ethnocentrism* or *logocentrism*. If we could create a unified concept of mankind (which has still to be proven), it would only be from a history of trace or grammè.

With the advent of machines and the digital era, the externalization of trace – this movement of differance that precedes all oppositions – is broadening. The possibilities of setting aside take on a new dimension. Trace or archi-trace for Derrida is a much broader "structure", which includes and makes possible the classic, oppositive concepts of *trace, sign, presence and absence, writing and speech*:

– trace no longer has a secondary relationship to the thing itself (*die Sache selbst*): trace is "first", "original";

– but precisely, primacy and origin no longer make sense, by the very act of saying this;

– trace is not "the mix" between presence and absence, nor the "passage" between presence and absence, nor "the presence of absence", nor a dialectic between presence and absence,

– trace evades this opposition and *"makes it possible from the irreducibility of excess"*.

Any trace can always be erased, be forgotten, be lost or disappear in some way. This loss belongs to this structure. However, archi-trace is already erased. On the one hand, it has already disappeared into forgetting; it no longer exists. However, it has never existed or, more exactly, it appears only to be erased (and it if succeeds, it is only in being erased).

However, "*the erasing of trace*" does not mean "*erasure*" (the action of voluntarily erasing): indeed, no one can ensure that a trace can be definitively and totally erased. Trace can always return as a symptom, a ghost or otherwise (unexpectedly, unpredictably, monstrously or unimaginably).

For Derrida, we are, and always remain, haunted by trace, its possible, unexpected re-appearance. This distinction that we will use after reading Derrida between "erasure" and "effacement" of trace takes on its whole meaning once again with digital traces. Even if Derrida does not suggest it, this distinction nevertheless seems to us to integrate into Derridian taxonomy the oppositions, neologisms and other possible and contradictory paleontologisms, which they could have used to describe trace in the digital era especially.

For Derrida, at this particular instant, without place, nor meaning, nor referent, where trace has become ash, we cannot even speak. Even negative theology can say nothing about it. The work only communicates with it in its erasure. In addition, nevertheless, we speak of it, it has been necessary to speak of it, even without saying anything about it. Even when it has disappeared, it is at work. Trace remains heterogeneous, irreducible, impregnable, sealed, unutterable and complex. Trace brings us face to face with the anguish of the erasure of the self, with the loss of all presence, with the possibility of the erasure of trace, which conveys its fragility, its vulnerability: digital trace, like any material trace, is a blatant example of it.

As soon as there is experience, as soon as there is living, as soon as there is a reference to the other, there is trace; it is the limitless basis on which writing, the stroke, the giving and the archive, etc., are inscribed. From the first trace (in the unity of a double movement of *protention* and *retention* in Husserl's meaning of these two terms), the text is a double one. By repeating itself, reiterating itself, the mark of the trace reiterates the event and the appearance. The invention, as it is defined in the modern world, systematizes this movement.

In the concept of trace, we have seen different problems in the meaning of contemporary philosophy converge:

– Levinas' definition, which is without doubt closest to Derrida's: "*a relationship to the illeity just as to the alterity of a past that has never been and cannot ever be lived in the form of the presence*";

– The Heideggerian intention, which Lévinas would abandon but to which Derrida continued to refer, for example in *Marges* and at the end of his article on *differance*;

– Nietzsche's position, in which the notion of trace (*Spur*) is irreducible.

Trace is outside of time and memory and is not spontaneous: it is outside of psyche. It is *"an additional machine, which is added to the psychic organization to compensate for its finite nature"*: in other words "a technè".

Derrida, analyzing Levinas' writing from the formula *"he will have obligated"*, enquires about this "he" who is entirely other, and calls us to responsibility for others. Invented in Levinas' own work, at this same moment, this total other is neither present, nor visible, nor pronounceable. It withdraws, and we must withdraw before it, in a series of crossings out (or withdrawals) that Derrida calls *"seriatures"*. *Seriature* is the abyss, a series of erasures that leave no trace, an archi-trace identifiable in the future perfect.

Derrida and Levinas mention the passivity of time and question phenomenology and ontology. They consider temporality as the movement of a radical alteration.

Derrida and Levinas stand together on the question of trace and the critique of Husserl's living present. Levinas pays this homage to Derrida:

[it is] *"the most radical critique of the philosophy of being for which the transcendental illusion begins at the level of the immediate. One can ask before the intellectual rigor of the voice and the phenomenon, whether this text does not cut a demarcation line, similar to Kantism, traditional philosophy, whether we are not, again, at the end of a naivety, awakened from a dogmatism that slept at the basis of what we took for a critical spirit. The finish, though to the end, of metaphysics: these are not merely hinterlands that have no meaning, it is the world spread before us that is incessantly revealed, it is the lived experience that is adjourned in experience. The immediate is not merely a call to mediation, it is a transcendental illusion. The signified, always to come in the signifier, cannot take shape, the mediation of signs is never circumvented. A view that agrees with what is, perhaps, the most profound discovery of*

psycho-analysis: the dissimulating essence of the symbol. The lived experience would be repressed through the linguistic signs making the texture of its apparent presence: an interminable game of signifiers setting aside forever – repressing – the signified" [LEV 98].

Levinas, echoing this tribute to Derrida, wrote in a fundamental text: *"trace as trace does not only lead to the past, but is the passage even to a past more distant than any past and any future, which still range in my time, to the past of the Other where eternity is drawn – the past absolute that unites all times"* [LEV 98].

1.4. Critical analysis of the concept of "digital trace"

Although there is strictly speaking no precise definition of the concept of *"digital trace"*, we have identified attempts in the literature at "transposition" of the concept of "trace" as we analyzed and tested in the previous pages regarding the digital era. *"The emergence of these new objects that constitute digital traces contributes to a renewal of the domain of trace studies. This renewal is however subject to a particular contingency in the digital context. In particular, it requires asking, in a historical and epistemological perspective, about the place of the digital in our contemporary societies. In fact, today there still exists no precise, commonly accepted definition of the notion of digital trace"* [GAL 13].

A definition of "digital traces" that could be termed "categorical" is suggested by the World Economic Forum as Mélanie Dulong de Rosnay recalls: *"according to the World Economic Forum's typology, traces of human activity in the digital world indicate the data created by and about individuals. They include: voluntary data, created and shared explicitly, by individuals, for example commentaries and contributions on social networks; observed data, resulting from the involuntary logging of activities, for example users' geolocation data from their telephones, browsing history; and data inferred about individuals, based on analysis of our voluntary or observed data, for example evaluation of solvability, judging age and social origin from a first name"* [DUL 17]. However, there too this definition is only a list of the different types of "digital traces" and in no case is it a true definition in the semantic or philosophical sense of "digital traces".

Dominique Cardon distinguishes the "*signal*" of "*trace*", as such, in the digital universe: "*to explain these differences, it is necessary to separate within proliferating big data, the data that suggest explicit content, subjective information or expressions, we call these data 'signals' (for example a status on Facebook) and those, implicit, that are contextual recordings of behavior, we call these data traces (clicks, geolocation, browsing, reading speed, etc.). The most efficient web algorithms are those that directly pair data signals with traces of behavior or, in other words, which make use of traces to find the best relationship between signals. However, when calculations are applied to signals without traces or to traces that little refer to signals, they do not have the same efficiency. Services that succeed in creating a learning loop between signals and traces have the characteristic of processing in real time information that is not found in the computer's calculating rules, but which is lodged, below the web, in the user's behavior*" [CAR 15].

Cardon thus opposes data which he calls "*signals*" and which correspond to "*subjective traces*" left on the canvas or on social networks by individuals (as commentary), against "*explicit traces*" that correspond in reality to what is normally called "*metadata*".

Metadata make it possible to describe data used in analysis and decision-making. They indicate both the exact definition of data in the semantic sense, as well as the data source (time, date, etc.), the exact manner in which they are calculated, aggregated and analyzed, and the professional rules that relate to them, from their process of extraction, transformation and loading to their archive, storage and even graphic visualization. Metadata play a crucial role in digital data analysis; thanks to techniques for searching, extraction, categorization and refinement applied to big data, *data mining* is enriched by all the algorithmic techniques resulting from all branches of applied math (statistics, algebra, stochastics, the study of probability, etc.).

In the definition suggested above by Cardon, there is also confusion within the terms about the use of algorithmic (complex) combinatorics, which are not limited to the use of one or more algorithms by these same actors on the web: to be able to categorize, pertinently, all hypertext links in a hierarchical and customized way, Google embeds billions of lines of IT codes analyzed by tens of complementary and different algorithms from the single, unique algorithm known as "*PageRank*".

It would be naive to think that the giants of digitization, such as Google, Facebook and Amazon, are content to use a family of algorithms or a type of *"self-learning"* (or *"machine learning"*) algorithm or another type of *"deep learning"* algorithm to optimize their results. Their power lies in the art and engineering of a large number of complex combinatory algorithms that rely on a plethora of data collected and analyzed in quasi-real time by a multitude of calculation rules in distributed mode.

Alain Mille gives a simple but fair definition of *"digital trace"* from the concept of *"trace"*: *"if we return to the general definition of trace, making it specific to the digital instance, the corresponding definition would be: digital trace is formed from digital imprints left voluntarily (or not?) in the IT environment during IT processes. Multiple findings show specifics linked to the digital character of traces: inscribing a digital imprint involves a digital coding and inscription of the code in the IT environment; digital traces such as digital imprints are inscribed in the IT environment: the IT environment is therefore the support for memory and the support for calculating traces such as imprints; the IT environment possesses (a) clock(s) linked intrinsically its technology"*.

Mille certainly reduces the digital to IT, but the transposition is not however uninteresting. He suggests a passage, a transposition of "trace" to "digital trace" made possible by the digital environment itself, with Simondian and Stieglerian accents (on the role and interdependence of the environment and technical objects). The world of digital calculation, IT support and memory are the specific conditions for the possibility of digital trace. The digital environment is at once the *medium*, the *substrate*, the *time* and the *horizon* for any digital trace.

What makes all the difference between trace in the sense of *"natural trace"* (produced by a living being in its biotope) and digital trace in the sense of an *"artifactual trace"* (produced by an artificial being such as a machine, a computer or even a program) is clearly envisaged and understood here: *"the inscription of a time stamp is always possible at the moment of imprint; the fact that imprints and traces are digital allow the processes of memory and calculation, giving them a character that is homogenous and coherent by nature. It is always possible to make new digital traces with existing digital traces (new interpretations) and eventually to return to the imprints themselves, provided that they are available in the same IT environment. The digital world therefore potentially normalizes the production of traces from imprints whose inscription is more or less controlled".* [MIL 13].

Digital trace, defined as *artifactual trace*, can not only be *"manufactured"* from any part, but can also be *"transformed"* voluntarily or involuntarily by human and/or technical intervention in its content itself, thus modifying its nature, or even its technical data, *metadata* that can be corrected or falsified fairly easily (the date and time of an email, for example).

The question of the veracity of data is fundamental here for understanding the challenge created by digital data and the challenges posed for data scientists. We addressed these points in 2015 in several articles, tackling the challenges of massive data and the role and growing use of fictitious data [BER 16, BER 13, BER 15].

It can also be considered that the risk inherent in falsifying digital traces is a specific risk for the integrity of digital traces, because in addition to erasure and the ease of deletion, is the possibility of the voluntary *corruption* or *alteration* of digital traces. We pass from *fictitious data* to *falsified traces*, and then to *fictitious digital traces*!

Louise Merzeau asks for the digital environment to be planned, to allow humanly acceptable management of digital traces [MER 13]. Digital traces are in essence objects for calculation whose intentionalities are questioned. Unlinking is inherent to the tracing process of producing traces immediately aggregated to other data and reinjected for new calculations taking place in the digital environment, and this happens continuously.

The concept of Derridian *differance* that we commented on above makes it possible to explain the process of memory reappropriation of digital traces. Indeed, we should distinguish and differentiate elements of digital trace in construction. To facilitate the circulation of such digital traces consciously formed in this way, Louise Merzeau suggests adopting a system of *"identity commons"*, and to achieve it, she specifies that: *"the principle is not to close off the use of traces, but to restore intelligence to the process"* [MER 13].

Mankind has constantly extracted and analyzed the flow of traces, from the earliest times to the digital era, when it became both the producer and the actor and where it now interprets digital traces; it is itself constructed by the same traces that it has produced, left, modified and sometimes erased. Beatrice Galinon-Mélénec goes so far as to suggest the concept of "Human-trace". Humanity, as a builder of traces is justified by the fact that, from the earliest moments of conception until the end of life, it is interactions with the environment that develop cognition [GAL 13].

From Shannon's information theory, via Wiener's cybernetics and theories on the *naturalization of consciousness* and *intentionality* (philosophy of mind and cognitive sciences), for some years we have aided, in line with Fred Dreske's concept of biological information, a shift in meaning of the definition of the subject (the individual) reduced to a program of *information naturalization* or the *biological reduction of information*.

Rejection of a semantic/philosophical definition of information means that any living organism processes information and could thus be reduced to a natural data processing system (by analogy with machines), reducing individual, personal ontology to informational meaning. With the acceleration of computers' calculating ability and the arrival of new IT paradigms (cognitive IT, cloud computing, quantum IT), enabling the processing and analysis of *megadata*, all disciplines (medicine, genetics, biology, etc.) contribute to carrying out the project of reducing the individual to their data (automation, molecular reduction, etc.).

What can be summarized by a last attempt at natural reductionism or of informational reductionism proves to be invaluable for understanding, nevertheless, cybernetic thought according to which any living being can be assimilated into a data processing system; from a living being's many physiological, behavioral and genetic traces, it becomes possible to contain all of the information relating to its traces on a digital support and thus create its informational heritage.

In our doctoral research from 2016 [TEB 16], published in full in a book that appeared in April 2017 [TEB 17], we tried to define digital traces as follows: *"digital traces are so many expressions or perceptions left consciously or unconsciously by their authors, left behind them at random and/or by chance: we speak of 'shadow information'. These 'phantom data' are formed by the set of data associated with a subject, an individual, a place, an event, and thus come to feed the data flow, the noise, that each Internet user makes on the web and social networks. Metadata formed by digital traces are therefore favorable to the analysis and extraction of meaning on the web and social networks".*

We reach the end of this chapter after recalling and analyzing unfruitful and unsatisfactory attempts at defining the concept of *"digital trace"*. In fact, no author to this date can meet the conceptual demands imposed by a rigorous philosophical approach to *"digital traces"*. The definitions we have mentioned are incomplete and truncated and they do not touch on the essence of the categorization, analysis or interpretation of data in the Big Data era, and their interactions with the individuals that we are: all producers, transmitters and receivers of data and metadata.

The syntagm *"digital trace"*, thus formed on a simple transposition of the concept of *"trace"* to the digital context and universe, cannot reach an *onto logical* nor even ontic meaning; in other words, the expression *"digital traces"* does not fulfill any valid semantic function. The terms thus linked do not refer to any truth function, or any truthful description of the world that they are supposed to express and mean together. As Carnap says [CAR 10], when we use a *"false-statement"*, we find ourselves confronted with statements with words that, taken separately, do indeed have a meaning, but that are used in such a way that no real meaning results from them. We see that the syntagm *"digital trace"* suffers from two major problems regarding philosophy: the statement itself, that is, the expression formed, and the invalidity of its definition, as it does not touch on the world and the object that it is meant to describe.

"Digital traces" do not in any way describe the reality and complexity of the relationship between data and its authors. We believe that the production and proliferation of data and metadata result from human interactions with the systems with which we form interfacing, interconnection, exchange and transaction, etc. relationships.

These human relationships with digital machines and the production of big data as a consequence can be defined as algorithmic projections in the sense of *"data and metadata production resulting from a human operator's interactions with the systems that surround them. Through its elementary formalization, it makes it possible to generalize the fluid notion of digital traces produced voluntarily or not by an individual. We take the example of a Twitter message written by a user of the social network. Its author believes they have only used 140 characters and that they are therefore able to control them. However, more than 4000 characters are actually sent. The difference lies in the set of metadata that accompanies each message (user account, IP address, date and place of transmission, etc.). Again, this is a voluntary step, a conscious transmission taken by the individual...*" [BER 13]. These "*algorithmic projections*" form the long trail of diffused, entire, uncertain and sometimes contradictory data, which fashion as a digital IT train or "*digital data exhaust*", itself formed of imprints, signs and inscriptions of all the digital traces.

Here, we take an epistemological perspective inherited from the Vienna Circle's philosophy and a certain "*logical neopositivism*": "*a theory according to which any knowledge is only knowledge so far as it is formal, and consequently, extracting knowledge from its linguistic expression amounts to formalizing this expression logically, i.e. reformulating it in the canonical language of knowledge, formal logic*" [BAC 00].

The following chapters will make it possible to precisely define the concept of "*algorithmic projections*" and to give an initial mathematical formalization of the concept to show its entire logical articulation: "*as only modern symbolic logic is able to reach the precision needed in definitions of concepts and in statements, and to formalize the intuitive processes of inference from ordinary thought, i.e. to put them into a strict form, controlled automatically by the mechanism of signs*" [SOU 85].

2

Formalism Associated
with Algorithmic Projections

Cyberspace is a complex, dynamic and heterogeneous dominion with fluid boundaries. Its geography obeys subtle tectonics resulting from human calculations and emphasizes interactions in digital ecosystems whose complexity is only growing [KEM 12]. Professing to study it means above all making a choice of approach, which is not exhaustive and is by nature reductive. The angle of an IT or networks specialist is not that of an economist, or a specialist in geopolitics or futures studies. Each of these perspectives should be taken into account and included, while accepting their limits and the biases produced [ARQ 93]. It is from superposing different representations that an acceptable image faithful to cyberspace can emerge. Of composite nature, its topology results from a stratification of three layers that interact constantly and distort one another [DOS 11]. Structurally, a physical stratum can be identified uniting the network's physical framework, servers, routers, interconnections and machines supporting calculation, like a machine in Turing's sense. The second stratum is formed from all the programs, man-made or system codes, and more or less independent software run on the first layer. This stratum is called algorithmic; its informational nature is compatible with a formal description. The human calculation stratum completes the structure. It is a creating layer that engenders, sculpts and supervises the first two. Today, it is the only creating stratum in the stratification, awaiting future autonomous calculation systems, free of any human aid, and themselves codes generators. Cyberspace's systemic approach may be a route to access its complexity, while still bearing in mind the limits of perception and the realm of pertinence for such a direction. This approach should enable us to define some basic invariants playing a major role in data transfers in cyberspace. The algorithmic projection of an individual deciding to run an algorithm on a system is a data exchange component situated at the interface of human and artificial calculation. It contributes to the enrichment of their global algorithmic projection.

In 2020, the global volume of digital data will be more than 40 zettabytes. This exponential evolution triggers a general reflection on these new deposits' mode of use. In each of our digital interactions, we transfer a set of data into cyberspace, which will be backed up on archiving systems. It is from this statement that we suggest an unpublished formalism for this information in the form of algorithmic projections. We thus define the projection of a human operator in relation to an algorithm run on a system. This is broken down into open and closed components, then into voluntary and purely systemic components. Grouping projections creates S-projections and our global algorithmic projection, which forms our digital reflection. The projective formalism, applied to massive data structures, makes it possible to define bases for projection that are used in technologies for collecting and analyzing "big data".

2.1. Projective formalism

The concept of algorithmic projection was introduced in 2013 [BER 13] to describe the production of data and metadata, resulting from a human operator's interactions with the systems that surround them. Through its basic formalism, it makes it possible to generalize the fluid notion of the digital traces produced voluntarily or not by an individual on a system. Writing a message on Twitter is still a voluntary step of the individual, a conscious transmission. However, each time the individual crosses a town, they pass beneath the intrusive gaze of CCTV cameras; when they go through the subway turnstile, they trigger multiple sensors that enumerate their activity. An ever-growing proportion of their actions are thus captured by an observation system that increases their algorithmic projection without them being aware of it. Thus, a given individual's algorithmic projection is much greater than what they believe they transmit through conscious use.

This notion of digital traces as it has just been described suffers from a lack of reference regarding who produces these traces and the system that contains them. The concept of algorithmic projection makes it possible to remove some of the uncertainty linked to traces by relying on three entities at the root of the creation of a digital trace: an individual, whom we will call H, an algorithm A and a system S. These three components will make it possible to define the algorithmic projection written as P_S (H/A) of an individual H on a system S according to an algorithm A. Before this, it makes sense to agree on the given meaning of the terms "algorithms" and "systems" involved in defining an algorithmic projection.

Algorithm: we will call algorithm A any finite set of well-formulated instructions that make it possible to solve a problem. This definition underlines the fact that the algorithm ends by providing the solution after a finite number of calculation stages. When these run instructions after instructions, the algorithm is called sequential. If, on the contrary, all the instructions can be carried out at the same time, it is called a parallel algorithm. When the algorithm launches tasks running on a network of processors, it is called an algorithm. Its implementation consists of writing all the operations it is made of in a fixed programming language. The program obtained should be seen as a translation of the algorithm into the chosen language.

From a theoretical point of view, all algorithms can be matched with all calculable functions in Turing's sense. The Church-Turing thesis fixes the definition of calculability by describing its correspondences. In its physical formulation, it expresses the fact that "*the physical form of calculability, meaning any systemic treatment that can be carried out by a physical or mechanical process, can be expressed by a set of calculation rules, defined in several ways, which have been mathematically proven to be equivalent. In the so-called 'psychological' form of Church's thesis, the intuitive notion of calculability, which is connected to what a human being considers to be effectively calculable or not, can also be expressed by these same sets of formal calculation rules*". The Church-Turing thesis confirms that each effectively calculable function (each effectively decidable predicate) is generally recursive.

In terms of an effective calculation method, our algorithm A consists of a finite set of instructions that are described using a limited number of symbols drawn from an initially fixed "alphabet" set. The algorithm A produces a result (an output) in a finite number of stages and can be followed or "unwrapped" by a human operator with only "paper and crayon". Finally, running algorithm A does not require intelligence on the part of the human operator except the intelligence needed to understand and run component A's instructions.

System: etymologically, the term "system" comes from the Greek word "sustêma" meaning "a coherent set". There are several definitions of it, including that of the economist Jacques Lesourne [LES 76] who considers "a system as a set of items in a dynamic interaction". For Joël de Rosnay [DER 75], "a system is a set of items in dynamic interaction, organized according to an aim". It will be noted that this definition, implying an organization according to an aim, is not applied to social systems that are built on a number of sometimes contradictory aims. A system, seen as a set of items interacting with one another according to certain rules, is determined by its aim(s) or objective(s), and by the resources it has for carrying out these objective(s). These resources, which are varied in nature (material, immaterial, human, natural, artificial), interact with one another and are able to modify the system state. The system's organization relies on a set of principles and rules that govern the behavior and functioning of the entities that form the system. The system's boundary makes it possible to distinguish it from its environment by fixing classification criteria. Once the boundary is defined, the system enters into interaction with its environment. A system can be open, closed or isolated, depending on its degree of interaction with its environment. A sub-system is a system included in a higher tank system. System typology distinguishes natural, artificial or social systems, organized hierarchically or in a network, sometimes with the emergence of structures appearing during their evolution.

For the remainder of this work, we designate by the system S the entire coherent set that unites calculation methods able to run an algorithm, data storage spaces and interconnected programs within a network infrastructure, and a group of operators supervising the whole. This notion of a system implies a strong coherence in its architecture, its connectivity of its components and its supervision ensured by a group of human calculations. When this group does not exist, the system is called autonomous. The system's morphology, its perimeter and its sub-components can change over time. The system's dependence on time t is thus implied in the notation used ($S = S_t$). It will be noted that both of these algorithm and system definitions remain compatible with cloud computing and virtualization. The connectivity of the system's components and its final coherence result only from rational choices made by the team supervising the system. Its topology and morphology do not at all modify the nature of data transfers and data archiving. The system definition is "adaptive" enough to be applied to large infrastructures as well as to more modest architectures. Therefore, a social network forms a system, including physical machines, and an algorithmic layer. A site dedicated to online sales or transactions through auction is considered as a system connected to an electronic payment system. A system can contain one or more sub-system levels.

Algorithmic projection: a human operator is written as H. A group of human operators is written as $\{H_1, H_2,..., H_n\}$. The actions of H on the system S result from one or more biological calculations carried out by H deciding or causing the execution of the algorithm A or the set of algorithms $\{A_1, A_2,..., A_k\}$ on S. The operator H provides, voluntarily or not, the input data needed to properly run algorithm A on S and then collects output data after the calculation phase.

When H decides to run A on S, or involuntarily launches its running on S, there is a mutual exchange of information between H and S depending on A. We write I_S (H/A) the information transmitted (voluntarily or not) by H on the system S during the running of A and I_H (S/A), the information transmitted by the system to the operator H after running A on S. The entities I_S (H/A) and I_H (S/A) are two finite sets of binary words. A binary word is a finite set of 0 and 1 resulting from an initial interpretable by H and/or S. The information I_H (S/A) forms the system's response to running the algorithm A, sent to the operator H which is capable of reading, understanding and using it. I_H (S/A) can therefore be considered as the result of the calculation linked to A on S.

The sets I_S (H/A) and I_H (S/A) remain for the running time of A on S and are reduced after running to a fraction of archived information on the system, including the metadata potentially created by S during the running of A. This dataset called algorithmic projection will be written as P_S (H/A).

DEFINITION OF AN ALGORITHMIC PROJECTION.– We call the algorithmic projection of an operator H on a calculation and storage system S depending on algorithm A and we write as P_S (H/A) the finite set of binary words archived on S, resulting from the running of A on S, decided or triggered by H.

The content of this set depends directly on the nature of the algorithm A, on the structure of the system on which it is run and a more or less confirmed desire for storage on the part of the operators supervising S. Thus, depending on the system and algorithm envisaged, the algorithmic projection may be empty or reduced to very poor residual information. It may also group all the information exchanged when running A on S.

Instantaneous algorithmic projection: projection P_S (H/A) also depends on the moment at which algorithm A is run on S since the system S's responses can vary over time in terms of the level of archiving or the level of metadata creation. The instantaneous algorithmic projection of H on S depending on A is written as P_S (H/A)$_t$.

Accessibility partition: algorithmic projection P_S (H/A) can be split into two disjoint sub-sets forming the projection's open component and its closed component.

The open projection written as PO_S (H/A) contains the information belonging to P_S (H/A) archived on S, accessible to any user or any exterior system. It is the open component and it publishes the algorithmic projection.

The closed projection written as PF_S (H/A) unites the binary words of P_S (H/A) archived on the storage units S, maintained privately and reserved for a single group supervising the system S (its administrators, for example, in the case of human supervision).

The algorithmic projection is then expressed as a disjoint union of open and closed components: P_S (H/A) = PO_S (H/A) U PF_S (H/A).

It will be noted that the content of the open and closed projections can evolve over time with a data transfer of the closed projective component to the open projective component.

The reciprocal transfer is less pertinent in sofaras it can be considered that information remaining open for a certain time retains its accessibility character via duplication or archiving by another system. Therefore, a datum's open character remains persistent in the face of a desire to change its status to that of private data.

The questions and polemics about the sovereignty of data relate more often to the content and control of closed projections than to the management of open components [BOY 12, ARQ 93].

Digital identity, which supports the same breakdown type in open and in closed projections, can be addressed as a particular case in the formalism of algorithmic projections.

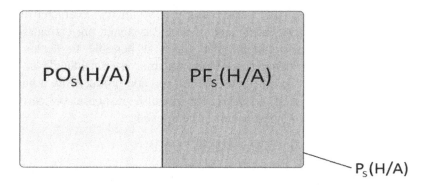

Figure 2.1. *Accessibility partition of the algorithmic projection*

Free will partition: a second partition should be envisaged from the angle of the conscious choice that the operator makes when they decide to run algorithm A on the system S. It is indeed a voluntary action answering a need, a desire or a lack of information. The data transmitted by the operator to the system and archived on S forms part of the voluntary projection. The operator agrees to entrust their data to the system and immediately loses exclusive supervision of it. This underlines the fact that the gain hoped for after running A on S largely compensates this supervision sharing.

At present, among P_S (H/A), we only consider the data transmitted voluntarily by H as well as the calculation results from running A on S from these data. This sub-set then forms the voluntary component of the algorithmic projection. It is written as P_{VOL-S} (H/A).

The additional sub-set in P_S (H/A) contains the non-voluntary or purely systemic information archived on S after running algorithm A. In the remainder of this work, it is written as P_{SYST-S} (H/A).

The algorithmic projection is therefore expressed as a disjoint union of voluntary and purely systemic components: P_S (H/A) = $P_{VOL\text{-}S}$ (H/A) U $P_{SYST\text{-}S}$ (H/A).

Depending on the nature of the system S and the algorithm A run on S, the components may be empty or may lack data content.

Classifying some data in the voluntary component can prove tricky in comparison with the difficulty of detecting the "voluntary" character of the information. It is therefore on the side of purely systemic projection where one must look for the argument that makes it possible to decide the connecting component: whatever is non-systemic is considered, in this partition, as a voluntary datum. Thus, the information produced by a human reflection, which may be a reflex, an impulse response or partially unconscious, is classified in the voluntary component.

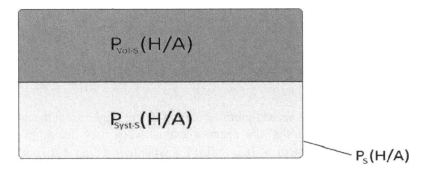

Figure 2.2. *Free will partition of the algorithmic projection*

By crossing the previous partitions, a finer partition is obtained, formed of four components:

– the open-voluntary projection PO_S (H/A) ∩ $P_{VOL\text{-}S}$ (H/A);

– the open-systemic projection PO_S (H/A) ∩ $P_{SYST\text{-}S}$ (H/A);

– the closed-voluntary projection PF_S (H/A) ∩ $P_{VOL\text{-}S}$ (H/A);

– the closed-systemic projection PF_S (H/A) ∩ $P_{SYST\text{-}S}$ (H/A).

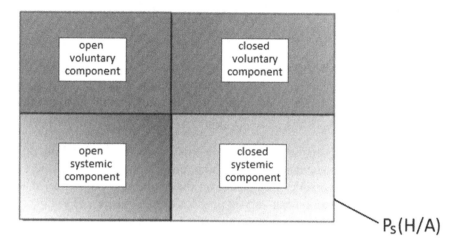

Figure 2.3. *Crossed partition of the algorithmic projection*

These components' data content is sometimes underestimated by the operator H, who does not have direct access to the last two projections because of their closed character.

It is often when a dispute arises, opposing the operator to the system, that one really becomes aware of the real challenges. It should be emphasized that the first two components participate very directly in developing the operator's "e-reputation", by feeding their store of public digital traces, archived on and outside the system S.

Information on the operator H, created by other players (individuals or organizations), figures naturally in their own algorithmic projections.

Their public components may be the subject of a search by H using a standard search engine or a specific algorithm. The data obtained are then aggregated within a new projection P_S (H/ A_{RECH}), where A_{RECH} is the search algorithm. The formalism of the projections remains entirely compatible with the notions of trace, digital identity and e-reputation.

2.1.1. An operator's algorithmic S-projection

DEFINITION.– We call the algorithmic S-projection of an operator H on the system S, the grouping of the algorithmic projections P_S (H/A) taken on all the algorithms that can be run on S. The S-projection is written as P_S (H) and verified: P_S (H) = U_A P_S (H/A).

By convention, when the operator H has still not run or triggered the running of algorithm A on the system S, the projection P_S (H/A) is empty. It will be noted that it can also be empty after the running of an algorithm leaving no trace on S.

An instantaneous version of the S-projection is obtained by considering the grouping of the instantaneous algorithmic projections P_S (H/A)$_t$, where t designates the time variable. Depending on the nature and properties of S, the instantaneous projection can vary in time following erasures, of voluntary or accidental modifications of the components' data. Data persistence is linked to robustness – the resilience of the archiving device on S.

Instantaneous S-projection: we call the instantaneous S-projection of an operator H on the system S, the grouping of instantaneous algorithmic projections P_S (H/A)$_t$ taken on all the algorithms that can be run on S. Instantaneous S-projection is written as P_S (H)$_t$ and it verifies:

$$P_S\ (H)_t = U_A\ P_S\ (H/A)_t$$

The definition of the S-projection that uses no time parameter proceeds from a time asymptotic approach. This means supposing that the system S is robust – resilient enough never to lose its data, or, when a major breakdown persists, for a preventive duplication to have been carried out on an external system. Cloud computing architecture is compatible with this type of "optimistic" hypothesis.

In the same way, modifying the algorithmic projection by the system itself is similar to running a new algorithm on S, which gives rise to a projection that will enrich the initial grouping. This strong and simplifying hypothesis makes it possible to discard the time variable by manipulating only the absolute set entities. The information contained in the S-projection of an operator H is not structured. Its organization results from an aggregation of binary words resulting from basic projections. It can include duplicates but it always reflects the intensity of the individual H's data interactions with S.

In the S-projection, an accessibility partition $P_S(H) = PO_S(H) \cup PF_S(H)$ is found, in which $PO_S(H)$ designates H's open S-projection H and $PF_S(H)$ its closed S-projection. There is also the free will partition: $P_S(H) = P_{VOL\text{-}S}(H) \cup P_{SYST\text{-}S}(H)$, where $P_{VOL\text{-}S}(H)$ designates H's voluntary S-projection H and $P_{SYST\text{-}S}(H)$ its systemic S-projection.

2.1.2. An individual's global algorithmic projection

DEFINITION.– The global algorithmic projection of an individual H is obtained by considering the grouping on all the systems S of the algorithmic S-projections. Written as P(H), this global algorithmic projection is written: $P(H) = \cup_S P_S(H)$.

An individual's global algorithmic projection should be perceived as their global digital reflection. It is broken down, depending on the accessibility partition, into open and closed components:

$$P(H) = PO(H) \cup PF(H)$$

then, depending on the free will partition, into voluntary and systemic components:

$$P(H) = P_{VOL}(H) \cup P_{SYST}(H)$$

H's global instantaneous algorithmic projection is written as $P(H)_t$ and it verifies:

$$P(H)_t = \cup_S P_S(H)_t$$

As a dataset, the global projection starts to grow at an individual's birth and stabilizes at their death. From a systemic point of view, the global algorithmic projection is empty at the individual's birth. It evolves and is enriched throughout their existence depending on their cyber-activity. An individual H who has no digital interaction in their entire life has an empty global algorithmic projection.

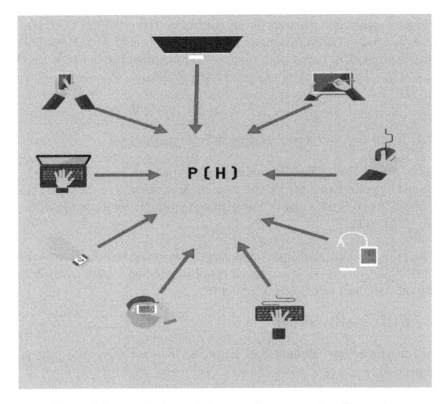

Figure 2.4. *An individual's global algorithmic projection. For a color version of this figure, see www.iste.co.uk/berthier/digital.zip*

The global projection P(H) grows depending on time, t. The archiving and duplication of data ensure this growth in volume throughout the individual's life. An individual's global systemic component is about to exceed their voluntary component in volume. The proliferation of connected objects and connected environments contributes to this tipping of the voluntary towards the systemic. This evolution should make us question:

To what extent can our free will accommodate a systemic global algorithmic projection? Should it be opposed? Each user of digital means develops their answers depending on their culture, education and cognitive biases. These responses depend on the individual level of algorithmic consent, which will be defined in Chapter 3.

2.1.3. *Big data and bases for algorithmic projection*

Projection basis: we call $G = \{H_1, \ldots, H_n\}$ a group of n individual users of the system S, deciding or launching the execution of certain algorithms on S. A is an algorithm run on S by each of the group's users. The algorithmic projections P_S (H_i /A) can be grouped in a database written as $B_{S,G}$ (A) called the projection basis of G on S depending on A and verifying $B_{S,G}(A) = U_{1 \leq i \leq n} P_S$ (H_i /A).

The content of this basis reflects the use by a group of users G of algorithm A on the system S.

By this time considering all the algorithms that can be run on S, the basis $B_{S,G}$ is built, grouping the S-projections of the user group G.

This basis is defined by $B_{S,G} = U_{1 \leq i \leq n} P_S$ (H_i) and is called the projection basis of the user group G on S.

The basis $B_{S,G}$ (A) is a data deposit pre-structured by the action of algorithm A run on S by the user group G. If the size of the group G is high (large n), the volume of the projection basis can rapidly become substantial and give rise to techniques for processing and analyzing big data (big data technologies).

The commercial use of projection bases is involved systematically in predictive analysis (where n is high) and in data visualization and it relies on creating aggregates in real time. Projection bases are used in "data-mining" architectures. The nature of the algorithm associated with projection influences the processes of data enrichment, "cleansing" or classifying the information collected. The study of frequencies, comparative analyses and the creation of "consumer behavior profiles" taking account of user's habits, influences and trends fit easily to the formalism of projection bases. Generally, the representation of a datum using algorithmic projection can improve its tagging in micro-targeting and can facilitate decision-making at low latency.

2.1.4. *Some examples of algorithmic projections*

Some canonical examples of projections associated with elementary algorithm families such as Print, Mail, Bid, Buy, Pay, and Crypt make it possible to illustrate the projective formalism.

Print algorithm: the family of *Print* algorithms designs any voluntary publication of a text, image, sound or video by an operator on a public or private viewing system. In concrete terms, this formalism covers the writing of a tweet, a public message on a discussion forum or on a social network, uploading a video online on YouTube or a photo on Instagram. Publication (Print) results from a voluntary act decided by an individual at a given date. The user H is aware of the "public" character of their information and wants first and foremost to be read, heard or seen.

The algorithmic projection P_S (H / Print) contains the message M, that is, the set of binary words I_S (H/ Print), as well as the metadata associated with it (date, time of sending, operator identifiers). The message posted by the user is archived on their personal account, so on the archiving system of S, sometimes with a great deal of ambiguity over the final control and supervision of this information. The user sometimes deletes (or believes they have deleted) the message from their personal area although it is kept in the storage zones of S without the user being alerted. The open projection component PO_S (H/ Print) also contains the message and some metadata, and the closed component PF_S (H/ Print) collects the metadata created by S but depends above all on the analysis and interpretation potential of the system running the publication algorithm. The voluntary component of the projection groups the entire message, while the associated metadata are archived on the purely systemic component.

Mail algorithm: the *Mail* family designs all algorithms associated with the voluntary sending of a message (text, image, video, SMS, etc.) by a user sender H to one or more recipients. It is understood that the operator does not want their message to be read by anybody except the legitimate recipient(s).

The message is in general momentarily archived on the email accounts of the senders and recipient(s). It can also be archived by any system (S or others) responsible for collecting and analyzing this type of data. The archiving, which is secret and automatic, is carried out unknown to the operator sender and will supply big databases often supervised and managed by state agencies. The eventuality of there being a systematic safeguard followed by an automated analysis arouses intense debates (the American surveillance system Prism, the revelations of Edward Snowden, the European Indect program) and is forcing the cyber citizen to reflect (and introspect) on the future of the data they send daily, voluntarily or otherwise. Algorithmic projection P_S (H/ Mail) can contain, depending on the nature of the system and its intrusive potential, only the metadata associated with sending the message but also those metadata accompanying the complete message in a context of generalized collection systems. The open projection component PO_S (H/ Mail) is in principle empty, but the entirety of the information in the message can reside on a closed component PF_S (H/Mail). The choice to encrypt the transmitted message or not does not modify the transfers of information between the system and the user. It imposes a cryptanalysis phase for the system that implements automated monitoring and surveillance of the email traffic. The nature and meaning of the information remain invariant, only the coding is modified. The voluntary component can contain all or part of the initial message, depending on the archiving policy developed by the system S.

The Bid algorithm: the *Bid* family designs any action on a commercial system supervising auction transactions. The projection P_S (H/Bid) then corresponds to the information archived on S (data and metadata) after a bid on the placement of a reference object for sale by S. The projection contains in particular the bid amount suggested by the user H and the identifiers for the object and operator. The archived information, even reduced to a simple bid amount, can prove "informative" with regard to competition from other bidders and the object's final sale price. The interest that the user has in the object appears naturally in the logical sequence of action, which does not exist in a fixed-price sale arising from a binary decision (I do or do not buy the object).

The series of projections on a complete cycle of bids made on an object placed on sale on S, written as { P_S (H/Bid$_1$), P_S (H/Bid$_2$), ..., P_S (H/Bid$_k$)} contains all the information resulting from the strategy implemented by the user H on the auction system. Depending on the system and choice of vendors, this projection series can be open or closed; in the latter case, only some metadata remain accessible.

Other algorithm families: e-commerce and online sales involve projections associated with the elementary algorithms *Buy* and *Pay*, for the sale of and online payment for an object or service. These contain the history of the transaction and metadata that make it possible to structure the information.

The *Crypt* family of cryptography algorithms used to encrypt sensitive information engenders a projection whose content can in its turn be used for cryptanalysis.

Finally, the *Crawl* family designs search algorithms carried out on the web using a search engine.

This formalism by algorithm type can facilitate the tagging of raw data in automated collection. If the data are identified as resulting from an algorithmic projection associated with A, its structure will use the algorithm's characteristics and will enable pertinent data aggregates to be formed.

2.1.5. The volumes of an algorithmic projection

A projection's raw volume: as a finite set of binary words, any algorithmic projection P_S (H/A) has a raw final volume. This measures the size of the data contained in the projection without putting it into any particular form and without compressing this information. The duplicates are therefore "counted" with their orders of multiplicity. In the remainder of the work, this raw volume expressed as a binary unit and its multiples will be written as $|P_S$ (H/A)$|$.

K-Volume of a projection: we designate a lossless data compression algorithm as K, applied to any finite binary word m. K(m) is the compression of m. For K to be an effective compressor, the length of l(K(m)) should verify l(K(m)) < l(m) for any binary word m. If P_S (H/A) = {m_1, m_2, ..., m_n}, the concatenation (according to a self-delimited encoding) of the projection words m = $m_1 m_2$ ... m_n is a binary word to which K can be applied. The compression of K of the algorithmic projection will be written as K (P_S (H/A)) = K(m).

DEFINITION.– The K-volume of the algorithmic projection P_S (H/A) is written as $|P_S$ (H/A)$|_K$ and verified: $|P_S$ (H/A)$|_K = |K$ $(P_S$ (H/A))$|$.

The K-volume is a measurement for the chosen lossless compression algorithm K, which makes it possible to evaluate the quantity of information contained in the algorithmic projection by deleting some duplicate data.

Mean compressed volume of a projection: if K_1, K_2, ... , K_P designate p lossless compression algorithms, we will write as:

$$\mu \ (P_S \ (H/A)) = 1/p \ \Sigma_{1 \leq i \leq p} \ | \ P_S \ (H/A) \ |_{Ki}$$

the average compressed volume of the projection P_S (H/A) relating to the family of compressors $\{K_1, K_2, ..., K_P\}$.

REMARK.– It is possible to build a measurement for the similarity in content between two projections from a lossless compression algorithm K. This measurement proves useful when we seek to class projections by degree of similarity, relative to compressor K.

2.2. E-reputation and algorithmic projections

2.2.1. Digital reputation

E-reputation, sometimes called digital reputation, web-reputation or cyber reputation, covers the shared opinions that form in cyberspace about a given individual or entity. This heterogeneous dataset emerges directly from digital interactions and data transfers diffusing between physical space and cyberspace. The projective formalism provides a tool for a systemic approach to e-reputation.

2.2.2. Brief history of e-reputation

In the mid-1990s, the first questions on the transfer of an individual's reputation to cyberspace appeared. They accompanied the development of video games and the first competitions between players who built their reputation from their gaming performances.

The notion of e-reputation appeared for the first time in 2000-2001 in an article published in 2002 by McDonald and Slawson [MCD 02] addressing "reputation on the internet". The authors used the context of a large auction site to illuminate the interactions at work between sellers and buyers on the system, the price of products and the role of emerging reputations. The indicators or markers from positive or negative evaluations (transaction history, public messages, number of stars) directly influence the formation of an object's final sales price and contribute to establishing the degree of confidence needed for the transaction. The reputation scores instill confidence and perpetuate activity.

The actual term "e-reputation" was used for the first time by Chun and Davies in 2001 [CHU 01]. They analyzed the emergence of e-reputation from diffusion compliance signals projected into cyberspace. These built and reinforced the reputation associated with physical space such as those that are installed on virtual spaces. The first systemic questions appeared at this time: how does one build one's reputation on, and by using, the Internet?

Between 2002 and 2005, numerous articles addressed methods making it possible to measure an operator's e-reputation from their activity on a system.

Problems with online commerce regularly feed these questions, applied to the seller as well as the buyer. Establishing confidence from digital signals is the subject of multiple articles addressing the optimization of marketing and sales performances.

In 2005, Chazaud [CHA 08] began a doctoral thesis, defended in 2008, on the links between strategic observation and the evolution of e-reputation. He studied the effective contributions resulting from data observation in mastering or controlling a business' e-reputation.

The period between 2006 and 2009 saw the multiplication of research and reflection on the subject, accompanied most often by the development of software tools for evaluating an entity's e-reputation. Numerous service providers, exclusively devoted to e-reputation, appeared during this period. These offer active observation services (opinion mining, setting alerts, mapping, influence analysis, community management), which enable the client to obtain an "instantaneous" snapshot of their digital reputation. The concept of e-reputation is first and foremost manipulated by its "practitioners": advertising agencies, marketing consulting agencies, print publishing and the media.

Since 2009, mediatization of the subject has led to a general awareness of the stakes of e-reputation: commercial, economic, legal, psychological and strategic. The notion of the right to be forgotten in digital space appeared as an immediate corollary of e-reputation and led to new legal and ethical questioning. Ever more integrated within the business' information system, the management of e-reputation today occupies a strategic position, uses specific technologies and plays a role in the creation of specialist jobs. While seeking to normalize and develop the management of its e-reputation, a business should take care not to become the victim of collateral biases created by this new entity. A business should in particular be aware that current functional limitations hold back automated e-reputation analysis tools (of a semantic nature). Finally, it should take account of the extreme volatility of a shared opinion expressed in digital space. The binary viewpoints (this brand is serious or not, this seller is recommended or not) collected from a big dataset are only a contextualized snapshot that it makes sense to illuminate in real time if we seek real, usable information.

2.2.3. An operator's systemic approach to e-reputation

An individual's e-reputation is established from their own global algorithmic projection (what the individual has produced about themselves) and from what other users of digital means produce on systems about this individual. This second component, of external origin, is distributed with the algorithmic projections engendered by these users.

In this section, H* designates a human user of digital means and D (H*) a set of denominations of the individual H*.

D (H*) = $\{d_1, d_2, ..., d_n\}$, for which each denomination d_i makes it possible to identify the individual H* without ambiguity (name, first name, digital identifier, specific function ensuring identification, photography, unique biometric imprint).

We consider the group of human users to have executed the algorithm A on S by producing an algorithmic projection P_S (H/A) that meets D (H*), such that: P_S (H/A) $\cap$ D (H*) $\neq$ $\emptyset$. This group of users is written as G (D (H*), A, S).

This set groups the operators that produced the information projected about H* on S according to algorithm A:

$$G\ (D\ (H^*),\ A,\ S) = \{\ H,\ P_S\ (H/A) \cap D\ (H^*) \neq \varnothing\ \}$$

It then makes it possible to define the projected information resulting from running A on S meeting the denomination set D (H*) by:

$$J\ (D\ (H^*),\ A,\ S) = U_{\ H\,\epsilon\,G\,(\,D\,(H^*),\,A,\,S\,)}\ P_S\ (H/A)$$

By considering the total, taken from all the algorithms that can be run on S, of this projected data, we define the projected S-information meeting D (H*) by:

$$J\ (D\ (H^*))_S = U_A\ J\ (D\ (H^*),\ A,\ S)$$

Then, by linking it on all accessible systems, we define the projected information meeting D (H*) by:

$$J\ (D\ (H^*)) = U_S\ J\ (D\ (H^*))_S$$

Set J (D (H*)) contains all the information produced by users, on the individual H*, meeting the denomination set D (H*). This set is growing through the addition of new denominations in D (H*).

As for an algorithmic projection, the projected data meeting D (H*) is formed of a voluntary component (resulting from the free will of different users contributing to it through the algorithmic projections), and a purely systemic component engendered when running contributing algorithms. We also find the free will partition separating the set into open projected data and closed projected data.

An individual H*'s e-reputation is formed by the feedback, in the open and closed components of the projected data meeting D (H*).

If the denomination set provides enough "coverage", J (D (H*)) contains, as far as data is concerned, the individual H*'s e-reputation. The previous construction makes it possible to sectorize this reputation according to several scales; at the most refined level by the algorithm defining the projections, then at the level of the system on which it is placed and, finally, at the global level of data production. The algorithm used, as well as the system, directly impact the type of data produced and projected (its volume, quality, variety, flow and pertinence). The projective breakdown gives access to the nuances of texture that form an individual's e-reputation.

2.3. Competition, hacking and algorithmic projections

2.3.1. Competition, duels and algorithmic projections

A conflict of rationalities opposing groups of human operators is projected naturally into cyberspace. It then creates competition situations or dueling algorithms [BER 13] that directly impact the content of algorithmic projections as well as their morphology. Feedback loops are installed, acting on different actors' projections. A cyber-attack targeting a data system triggers turbulence on physical and digital spaces and causes the production of algorithmic projections characterizing the attack.

The Trojan horse or Trojan is a program used as a vector to introduce one or more programs with their own function into a digital system: delayed takeover, destruction or sabotage of an infrastructure, duplication, modification or deletion of information. The Trojan has two components: an initial, public one that must seem innocuous, attractive and useful to the user and/or the system it targets and which exists with the sole aim of being accepted by the operator and/or system. The second private, secretive component contains the harmful, active algorithmic charge that will be deployed in the system after penetrating it and then making it possible to take whole or partial control of the system.

The installation of a Trojan could, for example, make possible the reading, modification or deletion of data or programs in the targeted system. Running the algorithm T containing a Trojan on the target system S most often results in an unfortunate decision by a human user H, fooled by the innocuous and useful appearance of T. The validation of the Trojan, which occurs only on its public and attractive part, triggers the running of the viral load on the target system. The projection P_S (H/T) that results often contains traces of the effects of the two components of T. The attractive, public part of the load is projected onto the voluntary component P_{VOL-S} (H/T), whereas the harmful part is projected onto the purely systemic component P_{SYST-S} (H/T). Once infected, the system S archives projections that can potentially contain traces of activity of the viral load T. Thus, part of the T's activity history features on the users' S-projections produced after infection. These will serve as a warning to the administrators of the infected system who will proceed, via new algorithmic projections, to neutralize T.

Other viruses V will seek to minimize their digital imprints on the S-projections to remain invisible on S for as long as possible. This is notably the case with spyware destined to collect information in the context of economic or military cyber-intelligence campaigns, while still maintaining a high level of secrecy within the target system. The viral agent deployed on the system will be secured to collect for the attacker's benefit any closed, voluntary or systemic algorithmic projection, archived on S. In parallel, an exhaustive search of open projections associated with the target will complete this quest for information.

Sometimes, the attacker's objective will be to modify or delete algorithmic projections on the target system. They must pair speed and secrecy to reach these while outwitting security shields on S. This dueling algorithm context will engender a duality of projections that each actor will finally seek to use.

2.4. The stakes for a projective data approach

2.4.1. *Structuring massive data using the projective formalism*

To be pertinent, a formalism should both facilitate the representation of complex interactions and play a part in illuminating relations, unknown similarities, hitherto invisible or scarcely visible on existing models. The projection approach implies a positioning situated at the interface of two calculation strata: that of human calculation and that of artificial calculation. This abstract zone, at the forefront of silicon computing and human strategies, is undergoing constant mutation [DOS 11]. The NBIC (nanotechnology, biotechnology, IT, cognitive sciences) convergence rapidly reduces the distances separating calculation supports. IT innovation is clearly evolving into a bio-digital fusion. It therefore appears natural to define formalisms compatible with this convergence.

The exponential acceleration of our digital data production, too, justifies research on the representation of data flow moving from physical space to cyberspace.

In 2012, the digital universe contained around 2,837 exabytes. In 2015, this global volume exceeded 8,500 exabytes, and it is predicted to exceed 40,000 exabytes in 2020, which will make 40 zettabytes.

In 2011, five exabytes of data were generated on earth every two days, while, in 2013, this volume was reached within 12 minutes.

The number of Internet users in the world increased by 18.5% between 2013 and 2015 to reach 3.2 billion users in 2016.

The following table shows the volumes of data and algorithmic projections produced in a minute by users on different platforms (sources: platforms, data 2016).

Large American platforms	Activity per minute (in 2016)
Skype	110,040 calls
Uber	694 clients transported
Facebook	4,166,667 users like a post
Twitter	347,222 tweets are sent
YouTube	300 hours of new videos placed online by users
Instagram	1,736,111 photos "liked"
Pinterest	9,722 photos pinned
Apple	51,000 applications downloaded by users
Netflix	77,160 hours of videos viewed by users
Reddit	Launch of 18,327 votes by users
Amazon	4,310 new visitors
Vine	1,041,666 videos viewed
Tinder	590,270 meet-ups
Snapchat	284,722 snaps exchanged
Buzzfeed	34,150 videos viewed

Unsurprisingly, the volume of activity on the Internet increased between 2016 and 2017. The second table shows activity per minute across all the large American platforms (GAFA and others).

Large American platforms	Activity per minute (in 2017)
Facebook	900,000 logins
YouTube	4.1 million videos viewed
Google Play & App Store	342,000 applications downloaded
Instagram	46,200 posts uploaded
Twitter	452,000 tweets sent
Tinder	990,000 Swipes
Email	156 million emails sent
Spotify	40,000 hours of listening
Amazon Echo	50 Voice-First devices shipped
LinkedIn	120 new accounts created
Messenger	15,000 GIFs sent
Snapchat	1.8 million snaps created
Online sales	751,522 USD spent online
Netflix	70,017 hours of viewing
Google	3.5 million requests sent on the search engine
Instant messaging	16 million texts sent

Activity per minute on large Chinese platforms is also growing fast. The following table shows the hyperactivity of large Chinese digital actors (BATX: Baidu, Alibaba, Tencent, Xiaomi) in 2017.

Large Chinese platforms (BATX and others)	Activity on the Internet per minute (in 2017) (sources: social websites cited)
WeChat	486 articles published
Miaopai	486,111 videos viewed
Didi	55,936 drivers accept passengers
DianPing	110 commentaries published
Taobao	13,888 commentaries published
Weibo	1,650,463 visits
QQ	11,111,155 messages sent
Baidu	4,166,667 requests sent on the search engine
Qunar	166 hotel rooms reserved
Zhihu	115,740 views
Ele.me	3,472 users made an order
Alipay	15,397,092 Chinese yuan paid

According to the report "China's digital economy" published in 2017 by the McKinsey Global Institute [MCK 17], from 2020, developing countries will produce more data (62%) than developed countries (38%). China alone will generate 22% of the global volume of data. These data will be linked to leisure, the general monitoring of physical and virtual spaces and the medical sphere. To data of human origin, there will be added data produced by machines: telephony, electronic appliances and connected objects. From today, the quantity of data stored in cyberspace about individual users exceeds the quantity of data they create themselves.

The projective model offers a partition in voluntary projection and in systemic projection that will make it possible to faithfully describe this duality in production as much at the "micro" level of a basic man–system interaction as at the "macro" level on projection bases. The association of a datum with the algorithm that engenders it facilitates its tagging and incorporation within a data cluster that is structured or being structured. Reciprocally, studying an algorithm covers its exhaustive description expressed in a formal language, a precise evaluation of its complexity in time and space as well as a validity domain fixing the type and ranges of data compatible with running a system. Its instability zones, if they exist, should be the subject of a precise location process [BER 13b].

Finally, the projection bases associated with an algorithm A that run on a system S contribute to understanding the interactions triggered, operating between the system and its users. The algorithmic projection ensures in some way "feedback" on the implementation of A and informs us about the responses of the system S.

On another level, a user's S-projections and their global projection open a field of study applied to interactive loops that can be installed between this user and their projection [VEN 09, VEN 11]. The data dynamic of these loops obeys forces of human origin (narcissistic impulses, emotional or educational want, addiction, militancy, mystic fervor, etc.). The users are forced to replenish their projection, which then operates as a public mirror and reflects an image filtered by the joint actions of the algorithm A and the system S. The loop is installed by feeding itself user–system responses. A concrete case illustrating this mechanism is that of an individual who self-radicalizes by frequenting extremist sites or forums. Radicalization is thus the corollary of the systemic loop [DOS 13]. Competitions or dueling algorithms [BER 13] give rise to similar mechanisms.

The collection and analysis of data for marketing, economic, strategic or surveillance purposes or for automatic threat detection can benefit from the projective representation of data. An individual's global projection contains by definition all their archived digital traces, each tagged by its generator algorithm. This projection may be targeted in a procedure for collecting information obtained from open sources (ROSO) [IFR 10]. Identification and the "study" of the target are interpreted by its global projection. The spheres for applying the projective formalism seem as many as they are varied.

Connected Objects, a Location's Ubiquity Level and the User's Algorithmic Consent

Although communication between two machines has been possible for some decades, it is only since 2010 that we have begun to witness a rise in connected objects designed to facilitate human activity and make the environment more interactive and "intelligent". The drop in the cost of sensors, the miniaturization of electronic components and an increase in connectivity, calculation power and storage are now making an exponential development in the Internet of Things (IoT) possible accompanied by the tsunami of digital data produced by these objects. As data producers, they transform physical space by creating a ubiquitous data flow (data available ubiquitously, all the time, in a transparent manner) between the environment and cyberspace. With an average outlook of 30 billion connected objects in 2020, the revolution of the Internet of Things is underway. Forecasts for the development of the IoT market and value creation in 2020 vary from one study to another, but they all generally predict an exponential progression. The connected object as a source of digital data fits fully into the formalism of algorithmic projections. The representation of a user's digital traces interacting with everyday objects and their environment makes it possible to define hitherto unknown concepts of a location's ubiquity level and algorithmic consent. Mechanisms for augmented humanity give rise to interactions and systemic loops created by connected objects and users as well as the algorithmic projections they cause.

3.1. The exponential evolution of connected objects for 2020

Defining the connected object amounts to considering any object with a wireless connection enabling it to exchange data with a computer, a tablet, a smartphone, another connected object or any device endowed with communication or calculation capacities. The term "communicating object" is also used to describe some connected objects. To date, there is no formal and universally accepted definition of a connected object. The definition used covers a spectrum wide enough to be applicable to a simple gadget or key ring connected to a car or an airliner that has several IP addresses [BEI 13] or to the autonomous ocean-going ship SeaHunter developed in 2016 by the American agency Darpa. Having said this, it seems more appropriate to speak of a connected system when we speak of a "big" connected object such as a ship, an airplane or a communication satellite. The connected object effectively occupies the entire spectrum of technological complexity, from the most rudimentary to the most sophisticated.

After they appeared in 1974, automatic ticket machines were considered the first connected objects. From this date, they have not ceased to increase in number. According to the Gartner office, in 2016, there were more than 7 billion connected objects, that is, more than there are human beings on Earth. However, it is difficult to predict precisely the number of connected objects there will be in 2020, as their growth is so fast and multidirectional. The Gartner office therefore estimates that 30 billion of them will be active on the planet in 2020, while Cisco Systems predicts more than 50 billion, connected to the Internet. The IDATE Digiworld institute proves even more optimistic, providing a prediction of 80 billion objects, which is the upper limit for estimates produced in 2015–2016. According to the Linley Group, the market for the Internet of Things (IoT) will exceed that for the smartphone from 2022. The global turnover of the IoT should pass from 1,928 billion dollars in 2013 to more than 7,065 billion in 2020. By relying on Gartner's study and average estimation, or even on that of the IDC think tank predicting 29 billion connected objects in 2020, it can be seen that the distribution of these objects runs the risk of demonstrating a high regional concentration – with 10.1 billion objects in Asia, 8.5 objects in Western Europe and 7.5 billion in North America, which forms more than 90% of the total.

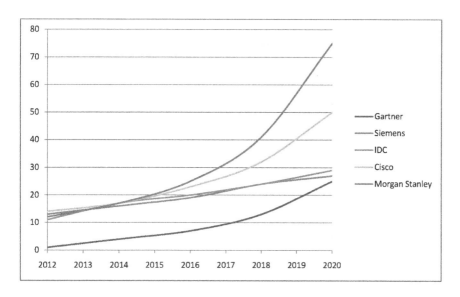

Figure 3.1. *Evolution of the number of connected objects over the period 2012–2020 according to several sources and think tanks: Gartner, Cisco, IDC, Siemens, Morgan Stanley. For a color version of this figure, see www.iste.co.uk/berthier/digital.zip*

Such estimations cover a spectrum of 10 to 80 billion connected objects in 2020, but portray an inability to precisely evaluate the level of consumer consent with regard to these sometimes "intrusive" objects, which are becoming producers and diffusers of personal data. Technically, the high estimation of 80 billion objects remains compatible with address coding standard capabilities that already offer an almost unlimited potential connectivity.

Massive connections have been made possible by the move to the IPv6 address coding standard. Replacing IPv4, which coded addresses on 32 bits, the IPv6 protocol now uses 128 bits and makes it possible to code up to 3.4×10^{38} addresses. This dizzying number opens up almost unlimited perspectives in terms of connectivity in the environment. It would make it possible to provide some 667,132,000 billion possible addresses per square millimeter of the Earth's surface! In practice, each square meter of the Earth's surface (including the oceans) has a minimum of 1564 IPv6 addresses, which makes it possible to envisage a hyperdensity of connections in the environment in the very short term.

On an economic level, the studies already cited show that the IoT's value added will increase fivefold between 2014 and 2020 and that this growth could impact French PIB by 3.5 additional points in 2020 [BAB 15]. The movement was clearly identified 4 years ago, the IoT's capital risk increased tenfold between 2010 and 2014, and the volume of the IoT's mergers and acquisitions increased threefold between 2013 and 2014 and then by three again between 2014 and 2015.

This progression relies on several vectors of growth, which combine to accelerate it. Among these vectors are the fall in the cost of sensors, the increase in wireless connectivity (4G to increase fivefold over the period 2014–2020), the increase in the power of processors according to Moore's law (sixfold increase in power between 2014 and 2020), the miniaturization of sensors and e-cards equipping the objects, the opening of storage space and IT processing (Cloud) at low cost. Transport, health, housing and industry will be the vectors most impacted by the influx of connected objects, especially in terms of value creation in 2025 (Figure 3.2).

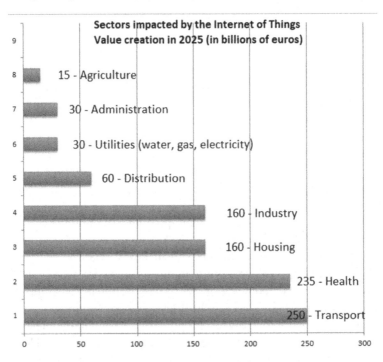

Figure 3.2. *Sectors impacted by the IoT and value creation for 2025*

Although 65% of French people still did not have a connected object in 2016, the 35% who did favored connected televisions, alarms and surveillance cameras, watches and bracelets.

Connected objects owned by French owners in 2016

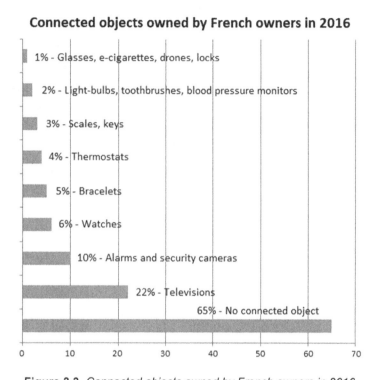

Figure 3.3. *Connected objects owned by French owners in 2016*

In 2015, more than 78 million connected objects of "wearable" type (objects, bracelets, watches, clothing, worn on the body, connected via mobile) were sold, thanks especially to the success of sports bracelets and connected watches. The "wearable" market underwent a particularly sustained growth from 2014.

3.2. Projective formalism applied to connected objects

A connected object is considered here as an entity producing digital data created by one or more sensors equipping the object. During its phases of operation, the object O runs a set of algorithms $A = \{OA_1, OA_2, ..., OA_n\}$ from captured data. When it is a very rudimentary connected object, it has no embedded means of calculation. Therefore, it merely captures raw signals or measurements that it transforms into digital data which it then transmits, via its connection, to its processing platform, for use. In this context, other algorithms B = { B$_1$, B$_2$,..., B$_p$} are run on the data by the processing platform supervising O, while A = {OA$_1$}, OA$_1$ is the only data transmission algorithm.

When the object O is more sophisticated, it can be endowed with a more or less substantial embedded calculation capability that enables it to run local algorithms, under the aegis of the processing platform and before transmission of the processed data (formatting data issuing from sensors, data encryption, data compression before transmission, etc.).

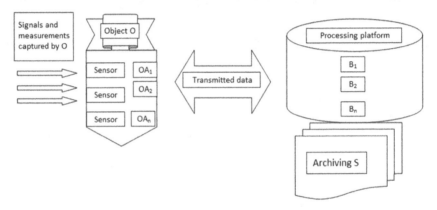

Figure 3.4. *Exchanges of data between the connected object and its processing platform*

The human user H of a connected object O generates the algorithmic projections: P$_S$(H/ OA$_1$), P$_S$(H/ OA$_2$), ..., P$_S$(H/ OA$_n$) and P$_S$(H/ B$_1$), P$_S$(H/ B$_2$), ..., P$_S$(H/ B$_p$) where S is the storage system of the processing platform as well as that of O, if O has one.

DEFINITION.– The algorithmic projection of a user H on S depending on the connected object O can be written as: P$_S$(H/ O) = U$_i$ P$_S$(H/ OA$_i$) U U$_i$ P$_S$(H/ B$_i$)

The projection P$_S$(H/ O) contains all the data produced by O during its phase of use by H, which are archived on S [BER 13].

The partitions described in Chapter 5 are applied again to $P_S(H/\ O)$:

– The accessibility partition $P_S(H/O) = PO_S(H/O)\ U\ PF_S(H/O)$ separates the open and closed components of the algorithmic projection associated with the object O.

– The free will partition $P_S(H/O) = P_{VOL\text{-}S}(H/O)\ U\ P_{SYST\text{-}S}(H/O)$ separates the voluntary and systemic components of the algorithmic projection associated with the object O.

By assimilating the connected object O with the set of algorithms it runs during its use, this object becomes compatible with the formalism of algorithmic projections.

3.3. A location's ubiquity level

The volume of the algorithmic projection of an individual H created on a system S according to an algorithm A is written as $v(\ P_S(H/A)\ )$. It can be expressed in bits or in bytes. We now consider an individual evolving in any location (an urban or rural environment, a more or less connected city [RAP 10]) over an interval of time [0.T]. During this period, they will produce voluntary and systemic (involuntary) algorithmic projections of which the total volume of the voluntary contribution is measured:

$$V_{Vol}(\ H\ ,\ [0.T]\ ) = \Sigma_{A,\ S,\ [0.T]}\ v(\ P_{Vol\text{-}S}\ (\ H\ /\ A)\ )$$

and the total volume of the systemic contribution:

$$V_{Syst}(\ H\ ,\ [0.T]\ ) = \Sigma_{A,\ S,\ [0.T]}\ v(\ P_{Syst\text{-}S}\ (\ H\ /\ A)\ )$$

The sums are taken on all the algorithms run by H on all systems during this period [0.T].

We then focus on the ratio of "voluntary/systemic" volumes during the period considered:

$$R(\ H\ ,\ [0.T]\ ) = V_{Vol}(\ H\ ,\ [0.T]\ )\ /\ V_{Syst}(\ H\ ,\ [0.T]\ ),$$

and then the mean value μ (R (H , [0.T])) of this ratio taken on all the individuals who frequent the fixed location during the period [0.T]. The location's ubiquity level can then be defined according to its mean value.

DEFINITION OF A LOCATION'S UBIQUITY LEVEL.– A given location is called ubiquitous at level N over the period [0.T] if:

$$\mu\,(\,R\,(\,H\,,[0.T]\,)\,) < 10^{-N}$$

The ubiquity level of a fixed location is the entire maximum $N_{[0.T]}$ verifying this inequality.

The greater N is, the more preponderant the systemic part of the projections over the voluntary part. This means that during the period considered, the location's density of objects, video surveillance systems and connected infrastructures causes this dissymmetry. The level N grows globally in an "intelligent" or ubiquitous city that is always highly connected (e.g. the ubiquitous city U-Songdo in South Korea [LEE 13, RAP 10]). The chosen duration of observation T determines a location's ubiquity level. We can therefore focus on the evolution of this ubiquity level when T tends towards 0. The limit is then interpreted as a given location's ubiquity level.

3.4. An individual's algorithmic consent

An individual's level of algorithmic consent relies in this case on a retrospective appreciation that the user brings to their own purely systemic algorithmic projection. The level of algorithmic consent (or consented ubiquity) in some way measures the degree of algorithmic freedom felt by users in a fixed location.

It is defined from users' algorithmic projections P $_{Syst - S}$ (H / A). Their projection production is observed purely systemically during the time interval [0.T] and then, at the moment T, they are asked to comment retrospectively on the acceptability of each of the algorithmic projections with the question: "You have involuntarily produced P $_{Syst - S}$ (H / A). If you had the opportunity to block or delete this projection, would you do so?" User answers then make it possible to separate the set of systemic projections created during the period [0.T] into two sub-sets: those systemic projections retrospectively consented to on the one hand, and those that are retrospectively judged unacceptable by the user on the other, that is, those they would have refused if they had the opportunity. Thus, the systemic projection on a system S over the duration [0.T] is written as: P_{Syst-S} (H, [0.T]) = $U_{A, [0.T]}$ P_{Syst-S} (H/A).

It is generalized to all active systems during the time interval [0.T] to obtain:

$$P_{Syst} (H, [0.T]) = U_S P_{Syst-S} (H, [0.T])$$

Then, we move to the retrospective user judgment phase, at the moment T, on their systemic projections:

$$P_{Syst} (H, [0.T]) = P_{Syst-consented} (H, [0.T]) \ U \ P_{Syst-refused} (H, [0.T])$$

This partition reveals the systemic algorithmic projection consented by the user on the one hand $P_{Syst-consented}$ (H, [0.T]) and, on the other hand, those which they would retrospectively refuse to produce if they had the opportunity: $P_{Syst-refused}$ (H, [0.T]).

By considering the retrospective volumes of these consented and systemic projections, we can then define the algorithmic consent ratio of a user in the city over the time interval [0.T] with:

$$R_{consented} (H , [0.T]) = V_{Syst-consented} (H , [0.T]) / V_{Syst} (H , [0.T])$$

Finally, the mean value of this ratio is defined μ (R_{cons} (H, [0.T])) taken over all the individuals frequenting the city during the period [0.T].

DEFINITION OF ALGORITHMIC CONSENT.– We call algorithmic consent over the period [0.T] or the ubiquity level consented to at a fixed location over the period [0.T], the value $C_{[0.T]}$ = μ ($R_{consented}$ (H , [0.T])).

The closer the mean value $C_{[0.T]}$ is to 1, the more algorithmic consent there is from users frequenting the fixed location. The closer this ratio to 0, the more users feel a loss of freedom and unacceptable recording of their personal data by connected infrastructure. The ratio provides a measure of the degree of freedom felt by the user within a fixed location over the period [0.T].

The value of the algorithmic consent depends, in particular, on the period over which it is measured and on the location considered. For example, the demand for automatic video surveillance systems seems much higher among the inhabitants of Songdo (South Korea) than in a connected European city. Above all, it is a question of culture, of risk perception and the acceptance of sometimes intrusive technology.

In South Korea, legislation on the "privacy and protection of personal data" is one of the least restrictive in the world (source Forrester 2016, Map – Data Protection laws around the globe). South Korean citizens tend to most easily accept the transfer of their personal data to foreign digital platforms. The number of video surveillance cameras belonging to government agencies is one of the highest in the world per number of inhabitants. South Korea is one of the top five countries globally with the highest rate of Internet penetration in the population (90% – source Internet worldstats, International Telecommunications Union 2017). In 2014, it was classed second globally for the rate of smartphone penetration in the South Korean population (source Statista Portal 2014). More generally, Asia, including China, represented more than 25% of the global market for video surveillance in 2017–2018 (source Statistica 2018).

Prosperity and development of an intelligent city: an intelligent city can only prosper, develop and increase its algorithmic capabilities if, when $N_{[0.T]}$ increases, $C_{[0.T]}$ also increases. In other words, the development and prosperity of a connected city rely on the joint increase of its ubiquity level $N_{[0.T]}$ and its algorithmic consent $C_{[0.T]}$.

3.5. The ubiquitous city, the generator of algorithmic projections

The smart city participates very directly in the development of its inhabitants' algorithmic projections. Interactions with sensor networks and connected objects present in the urban landscape contribute to enriching the global projection and in particular its systemic component. The volume of systemic algorithmic projection tends to exceed that of voluntary projection. This is a strong trend that can only be reinforced by the emergence of an ultra-connected ubiquitous city (U-city).

The concept of a ubiquitous city (U-city) relates to a hyper-connected city in which information is present, all the time, everywhere, accessible to all and invisible. The ubiquitous city has been able to integrate ubiquitous information in its architecture. It is built around a centralized data system (U-Media Center) that operates as the city's brain. The U-Media Center collects all the data issued from sensor networks implanted in the urban space, interprets them using Big Data processing algorithms, then directs the operation of connected machines according to the calculation results. This systemic chaining operates in real time, according to very varied space and time scales. The ubiquitous data is conveyed by a ubiquitous computing that is urbanized (the concept of "ubiquitous computing" dates from the start of the 1990s [BER 15]).

Thus, the data is spread both across everyday objects and behavior. According to Mark Weiser (Xerox Park), ubiquitous data corresponds to the third IT era. The first era was that of the Mainframe model: a computer and multiple connected individuals; the second era is that of the PC: a computer and a connected individual; the third era is that of U-computing: an individual and numerous accessible computers. Human behavior integrates ubiquitous data even more easily since ubiquitous computing is becoming transparent for the user. Ubiquitous computing is situated exactly opposite to the virtual reality that places man in the center of a virtual world resulting from digital calculation, whereas here it is a question of removing data and disbanding it across real space. The ubiquitous city "redocuments" its components at any scale of space and time.

The ordinary object produces the information and becomes a support and a document. Man's interaction with this object engenders algorithmic projections that in turn become data for the central data management system. The search for information and algorithmic mediation produces information. The contents fragment and undergo hybridization. All the city's business sectors are involved via the metamorphosis of its data space. U-shopping involves behavior using the consumer's algorithmic projections. Connected street furniture facilitates instantaneous nomadic access to adapted and personalized information. It takes part directly in the intelligent targeting of good commercial offers at the right moment [EVE 14, DAN 13, ACT 09].

In 2020, an intelligent city (Smart City) of a million inhabitants will produce a mean volume of 200 million gigabytes per day (one gigabyte (1 GB) represents a billion bytes). This production will result from all the infrastructure, interactions with inhabitants, objects and systems connected to the Smart City. The table below gives the mean volumes of data per generator type (sources Cisco Global Cloud Index, 2015–2020).

Data source	Volume produced per day	Ratio of data transmitted
Connected airplane	40 TB/j (1 TB = 1 Terabyte = one thousand gigabytes)	0.1%
Connected factory	1 PB/j (1 PB = 1 Petabyte = 1000 TB)	0.2%
Public security infrastructures	50 PB/j	0.1%
Weather sensors	10 MB/j (1 MB = 1 Megabyte = one million bytes)	5%
Intelligent buildings	275 GB/j (One gigabyte = 1 GB = one billion bytes)	1%
Connected hospitals, healthcare structures	5 TB/j	0.1%
Connected cars	70 GB/j	0.1%
Intelligent electricity networks	5 GB/j	1%

3.5.1. The example of U-Songdo, the first ubiquitous city

The concept of a ubiquitous city started to be applied with the U-Songdo project. Rising out of the Earth in 2003 on 610 hectares of reclaimed land on the Yellow Sea close to Incheon (South Korea) and 65 km west of Seoul, Songdo certainly offers the very first example of a hyper-connected ubiquitous city with sustainable development. This intelligent city now welcomes more than 76,000 inhabitants and concentrates around 300,000 jobs in one place. The cost of developing Songdo is estimated at more than 35 billion dollars and is supported by a private consortium formed of the project designer, the Gale International group (61%); a steel producer, the

Posco group (30%); and the investment group Morgan Stanley (9%). Songdo is first and foremost a concept of an ultra-connected intelligent city that is exportable and applicable to other geographical sites. This city aims to become a first-rate business center, a major technical research university and a city-laboratory experiment with the ubiquitous principle at its fullest extent. South Korea's highest towers can be found in Songdo, exceeding 480 meters.

The city was designed and built around a centralized calculation system, the U-Media Center, collecting all the data transmitted by the multitude of captors, sensors and surveillance cameras installed in buildings and urban furniture. The design of Songdo is unprecedented in the sense that the city's architecture is in perfect agreement with its global algorithmic projection. All the buildings have been "computerized" in their structures. Security cameras, omnipresent, film all urban activity in real time and enable, for example, optical recognition of license plates similarly to the biometric recognition of inhabitants. The collected data are continuously transmitted to the calculation system, the U-Media Center. They are then analyzed by sophisticated algorithms that produce and emit reviews, recommendations and forecasts intended to regulate traffic and flow. Ubiquitous information "accessible all the time, everywhere and for everyone" also serves to optimize the city's overall energy cost and to minimize its carbon footprint. The collected and analyzed data impact and influence the "ecological behavior of Songdo".

Built around a central park of 41 hectares, the city is well-equipped with cycle lanes, golf courses and river taxis. It has a metro that produces no CO_2 emissions, parking spaces are underground, rain is collected and filtered systematically and household waste is directed to the treatment center by a centralized vacuum system and then transformed into electricity. The buildings have green roofs and high performance solar panels. Each of them was built according to the LEED standard (Leadership in Energy and Environmental Design), that is, to high environmental quality. Energy optimization is calculated in real time by the U-Media Center which permanently regulates and adapts urban infrastructure according to its goal to minimize consumption. The ubiquitous city is inspired by biomimetics and seeks to reproduce ecosystems that integrate human technologies, thanks to green energy.

The American network giant Cisco has made Songdo its laboratory city and is carrying out numerous experiments on the site. Among these experiments in ubiquitous services, we find high definition medical and psychological consulting from home, with the best hospital consultants or even English teaching at home with American teachers. These services are particularly appreciated by Korean mothers with families who can both look after their children and enable them to benefit from the most competitive teaching on the market without leaving their homes. Digital infrastructure in Songdo is also favorable for remote working. Cisco supervises the U-Life system and its control rooms, permanently connected to all the apartments in the city. Finally, ONU has chosen to install the seat of its "Global Green Fund" at Songdo, a city that should see its population grow to reach 265,000 inhabitants in 2018, its year of completion.

China has just ordered its first ubiquitous "flatpack" city based on the U-Songdo model, from the American group Gale International. The Chinese market is logically considered as a priority by designers of intelligent cities. At a global level, Songdo shares the title of U-City with two other ubiquitous cities: Masdar, built by the United Arab Emirates in the middle of the desert on a budget of 18 billion dollars, which runs on 100% renewable energy, and Fujisawa which is currently being built and developed by Panasonic, south of Tokyo.

3.5.2. U-Songdo, ubiquitous city, or city of the future?

In each of these ubiquitous cities, it is the central calculation system that makes the city "intelligent". The more algorithmically effective this system is, the more "ecological" the city becomes, aware of its own resources and consumption. Interactions between cyberspace and physical space are then fully involved in the development of the intelligence of a city that knows how to exploit information to optimize its performance. A simple example is Fujisawa, whose public lighting system only turns on when sensors detect an individual's presence. It is therefore the individual's algorithmic projection that will contribute to energy saving and to the regulation of flow.

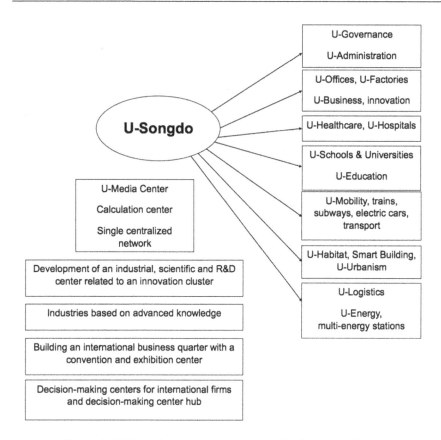

Figure 3.5. *Operational schemas for the ubiquitous city, U-Songdo*

3.5.3. *Predictive algorithms and feedback loops*

"Big Data" technologies make massive use of the user's algorithmic projections to optimize marketing [TEB 16], online commerce and the "intelligent" approach to the customer relationship. These projections feed many predictive analytics systems that aim to establish reliable predictions in random and volatile contexts. These predictive systems create a systemic loop, involving both the algorithmic projection and the user themselves. Predictive algorithms generally rely on using a continuous data flow (data streaming) to build predictions in the form of probable events linked to their probability of happening. Once analyzed, the data flow makes it possible to anticipate a trend, an evolution in time or a variable's future value. The main goal of the predictive algorithm is to maximize the reliability of the predictions it makes. An algorithm that is frequently "mistaken" would have no value and would ruin its designers' reputation. This algorithm therefore endeavors to remove random aspects and to favor a determinism that facilitates the user's interactions with their environment.

Predictive mobile applications can therefore prove very effective for predicting busy periods on a subway line depending on the timetable, location and data set collected in real time by sensors on a transport network. In this domain, the French startup Snips developed, in partnership with SNCF, the Tranquilien application in 2012. This application predicts which train lines in the Transilien network are most used and calculates which carriages we should choose to travel in for the most peace and quiet. Tranquilien's algorithms use SNCF data, Open Data and geolocation data produced by users' smartphones. These data are then crossed, interpreted and extrapolated pertinently to produce a prediction for the busy period which is updated in real time using information provided by travelers. The participative–collaborative aspect is an important component in the process of forming the prediction and contributes largely to its reliability. The prediction is then relayed to users who can take account of it before entering a carriage. Transport thus becomes more "intelligent" and more interactive. The example of Tranquilien perfectly illustrates the concept of a feedback loop that is implemented when a predictive infrastructure is activated.

3.5.4. *The systemic loop "data-predictive-action"*

The ultra-connected urban space thus becomes the actor in the forecast. It participates in a global movement that involves the removal of random chance. Feedback loops appear between the citizen using them in the connected city and the infrastructure. They are installed according to the following sequence:

1) The city produces massive data from users' algorithmic projections.

2) These data are analyzed by Big Data processing systems which provide predictions and trends in real time.

3) The city's users take account of these predictions, adapt their behaviors and actions, and then produce new algorithmic projections.

The sequence summarizing the systemic loop is summarized in Figure 3.6.

Data > Calculations > Predictions > Adaptations > Data

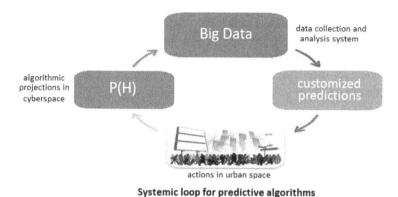

Figure 3.6. *Systemic loop "data-predictive-action"*

The systemic loop triggers permanent circulation of data resulting from users' algorithmic projections or produced by predictive analysis destined for users. This continuous data flow increases in volume and reinforces the ubiquitous data impregnating the physical space. The systemic loop therefore acts as a data generator at the interface of real and digital spaces. It plays the role of an active bridge between these two spaces while reducing a part played by the randomness that impacts real events. But only a part!

3.5.5. The limits of predictive algorithms faced with sheer chance

Predictive infrastructure can prove very effective on one type of random chance and much less so on another. Thus, the PredPol (Predit Crime in Real Time – Predictive Policing) algorithm system that was deployed in the city of Santa Cruz (California) in 2011, then in Los Angeles, Memphis, Charleston and New York in 2012 made it locally possible to cause a 33% drop in assaults and a 21% drop in violent crimes. The number of burglaries dropped by 20% in the city of Santa Cruz in only six months. From statistical data, PredPol was able to predict where and when the next crimes and misdemeanors were likely to occur. It will be noted that PredPol does not predict who will commit this future crime.

However, the predictive algorithm remains inefficient on "black swan type" random events studied by Nassim Nicholas Taleb [TAL 07]. Black swans are events with a very low probability of occurrence, very high impact on the system and which are retrospectively predictable. The concept of sheer chance described by Taleb relies on the existence of black swans, by definition outside of any predictive Big Data processing system. This form of sheer chance therefore persists at the heart of ubiquitous cities. "Soft Gaussian" chance responds fairly well to predictive infrastructure and recedes clearly under the effect of systemic feedback loops. The ubiquitous city for now retains this element of sheer chance.

The exponential growth of algorithmic projections from users of the "intelligent" city transforms the very fabric of the urban space. Ubiquitous data now covers the city by creating powerful systemic loops that operate between physical and digital spaces. Built on the ratio of the volumes of voluntary projections and systemic projections, a connected city's level of ubiquity makes it possible to measure and hierarchize its capacity to automatically produce digital data from users' activities. Other measures of ubiquity can be defined this time by relying on the effectiveness of predictive algorithmic infrastructure implanted at the heart of the urban architecture. The more capable the city is of limiting random chance and providing its inhabitants with reliable predictions, the more powerful ubiquity becomes. The development of turnkey U-cities, such as Songdo, by large building consortiums is now accelerating with new projects for which energy optimization challenges and random chance management challenges increasingly meet those of artificial intelligence.

4

On the Value of Data
and Algorithmic Projection

4.1. The complex problem of retrieving data

The projective formalism makes it possible to represent digital data D, which is known to be produced and archived on a system S after running an algorithm A launched by a user H. The data D is then written as an algorithmic projection of a user H on a system S according to an algorithm A: $D = P_S(H/A)$.

Let us now subvert the chronology. This time, let's consider digital data D about whose provenance, creation or generator algorithm nothing is known?

DEFINITION OF DATA RETRIEVAL.– The problem with retrieving data lies in determining, if they exist, its three projective components: a system S, an algorithm A and a user H, such that D is written as $D = P_S(H/A)$.

This amounts to being able to say by whom the data D was created, on what system and according to what algorithm. The problem of retrieving data is thus equivalent to that of this data's traceability. Its complexity is, by nature, high, given that raw data may contain no information on its traceability. Sometimes, on the contrary, the data content D contains all the information on its provenance and projective retrieval can be carried out with a high probability of (good) attribution. In all cases of retrieval, the projective triplet (S, A, H) is determined with a certain probability:

$$q = \text{Proba}\,[\,D = P_S(H/A)]$$

It will be noted that there is no uniqueness for the projective triplet (S,A,H) and that it is always possible for an operator H' to usurp the identity of the user H, to build a second system S' imitating S and an algorithm A' producing the same outputs as A while still being different. In this context: $P_{S'}$ (H' /A') = P_S (H / A) = D, projection obtained from a projective triplet distinct from the original. This possibility is often used in the social engineering phase of a cyberattack. The attacker steals the identity of a trusted third party to instill confidence in the target and lead them to click on a malicious link. The problem of retrieving data is intrinsically linked to the possibility of stealing the user's identity and producing false, imitation data. A chapter is dedicated to the structure of fictive data built and used in cyberattacks by HoaxCrash, BEC (business email compromise scam) attacks by false transfer order and cyber-intelligence operations. These families of cyberattacks all rely on creating false algorithmic projections to fool the target and induce them to carry out actions that will be profitable to the attacker. Used as vectors to intrude into systems, false data already occupy a central position in the architecture of cyberattacks.

4.2. How to define data value? The impact value and instantaneous value of interpreting data

4.2.1. An influx of data to develop

Data created worldwide exceeded 1.2 zettabytes (one Zo = 10^{21} bytes) in 2010 to 1.8 Zo in 2011, 2.8 Zo in 2012 and should reach 40 Zo by 2020. It is estimated that the global data volume doubles every 18 months. As an example, the social network Twitter produces 7 terabytes of data daily (1 To = 10^{12} bytes) and Facebook creates more than 10 To every day. The large radiotelescope Square Kilometer Array (SKA), which will be operational by 2024, will produce more than a billion Gigabytes of data per day, which is between 300 and 1500 petabytes each year (1 Po = 10^{15} bytes). The large hadron collider at CERN produces around 15 Po of data each year. The data volume produced by systems should soon exceed that produced by humans.

To tackle this data volume, big data technologies are evolving very quickly along three now classic axes, called the "three Vs" for volume, variety and velocity, which can be completed by two other Vs, visibility and veracity. The exponential increase in the volumes of data to be processed is leading to the creation of ever more effective "Data Centers" [TEB 14]. Variety, which conveys the heterogeneity of raw data that are often little structured, is usable by a complex algorithmic infrastructure capable of interpreting the data whatever its format. Velocity answers the need for speed in processing, which is ever higher, as well as data analysis in real time ("in memory" technologies) and "high frequency" digital systems. The sixth V could well involve the value of data, whether it is applied to a big data set or a simple tweet [BER 14, KEM 14].

Is there, therefore, an absolute definition of data value which is compatible with the environment in which it is interpreted or on the contrary, should it be restricted to a relative, local and instantaneous consideration of data? The study of concrete instances of transactions proves that data value remains a quantity that is volatile, temporal and highly dependent on the context on which it is evaluated. A systemic approach to the problem, based on a reduced formalism, makes it possible to define the instantaneous value of data in a context linked to the algorithm that interprets it.

4.2.2. Instantaneous value of data interpretation, impact value and sale value

The character relating to the notion of "value" obliges us to dissociate the negotiation price of digital data or a data set from its impact value in a context at a given instant. Two examples linked to hacking operations make it possible to illustrate this dissociation, which limits attempts at defining data's "absolute" value.

4.2.2.1. A 136 billion dollar tweet illustrating data's impact value

The Syrian Electronic Army (SEA) "cyber-war" cell appeared at the start of the Syrian conflict, in 2011, supported by the regime of Bashar El Assad. Between 2011 and 2014, it increased digital attacks against targets identified as enemies of the Syrian nation. Its first mission was to reestablish the truth on the Syrian conflict, in particular, from a structured counter-information infrastructure used on social networks (Facebook and Twitter), and on the Internet (through the website sea.sy). The SEA has carried out more than 200 cyberattacks against western digital interests of all kinds (media, TV, major American and European newspapers, European, American, Arabic and Israeli government sites, large groups such as Microsoft, Paypal, Facebook, Twitter and the US Army). These attacks rely most often on social engineering, intrusion (by phishing) and by hijacking an account from which the operation is launched. Targeted sites are regularly unlinked by redirection to a similar page containing a message, making demands and explaining the action. When levels of attack and the target's protection permit, the SEA proceeds to take control of sometimes very voluminous databases. Thus, during an attack carried out against the Forbes site in 2014, more than a million account identifiers were pirated. The attack on Paypal-UK made it possible to seize the service's online payment database. The SEA sometimes uses distributed denial of service attacks (DDos) or injects secret agents to collect more sophisticated information (spyware), in particular, against Syrian rebels for the purposes of cyber-intelligence.

On April 24, 2013, the SEA targeted the Twitter account of the American agency Associated Press (AP) [KEM 14]. It momentarily took control and at 13:07 published the following message: "*Breaking: Two Explosions in the White House and Barack Obama is injured*". 1.9 million followers of the Associated Press Twitter account received the fake message posted by the SEA, believing it to be authentic. The reaction on financial markets was almost immediate. Between 13:08 and 13:10, the main index on Wall Street, the Dow Jones (DJIA), lost 145 points, equivalent to 136 billion dollars (105 billion euros), due to panic among human operators, but also due to high frequency trading (HFT), which interpreted and "reacted" to the false tweet. Shares in Microsoft, Apple and Mobil dropped by more than 1% almost instantly. Some minutes later, Associated Press regained control of its account and immediately published a tweet declaring that the previous message was a fake and that it resulted from pirate activity on its account. Immediately, the Dow Jones index regained its entire value, which had just dropped, and rapidly regained its normal course. The short lifespan of the fake message published by the SEA was enough to alter a key stock market index. The activity of automated systems for high-frequency trading, capable of passing orders in a few microseconds, has modified decision-making lines, removing human control at the end of the operation.

Automatic validation and acceptance of false information can therefore have a considerable impact on an interconnected environment. We should query the real value of the SEA tweet, as data, considered as real at one instant and then denied a few minutes later. It is clear that this value depends both on the time variable but also on the validation that we wish to give it, and finally on the context on which it is interpreted. It is therefore necessary to agree on the meaning of the word "value": is it the best sale price of the data obtained by a seller from an operator-buyer or should one take account of this data's "impact value" in a more global context or environment? In the case of the false SEA tweet, the impact value would be high, since it should take account of the cost of turbulence on the markets during the data's validity period. That said, when the tweet's fraudulent origin was revealed, retrieval of this message's algorithmic projection made it zero-value data. The time factor and the confidence one places in digital data thus contribute greatly to its impact value.

4.2.2.2. The legal sale of customer data by Microsoft to the FBI?

In January 2014, a hacker unit from the Syrian Electronic Army targeted the official Microsoft site repeatedly and was able to seize databases, emails and invoices created by Microsoft to sell "customer" data to the Federal Bureau of Investigation (FBI). On January 21, 2014, the SEA published a copy of numerous Microsoft invoices sent to the FBI on its website as well as listing the personal data sold. This affected users of Outlook or Skype and contained the identity, identifier, IP address, hotmail account name and the passwords of online service users. According to invoices published by the SEA (and with the caveat that they were not subject to modifications or falsification), the unitary cost of a data set about a user varies between 50 dollars and 200 dollars depending on the content transmitted. For the month of November 2013 alone, the invoice created by Microsoft reached 281,000 dollars. The invoice for August 2013 reached 352,000 dollars. A data set containing the user password for a Microsoft product was charged at 200 dollars, the maximum tariff observed in the "leaks" published by the SEA. It will be noted that this type of transaction is perfectly legal when formally requested for use in a criminal investigation. Other invoices were created by Microsoft for foreign private societies based in South America when selling customer data. These transactions illustrate, concretely, our queries about data value. In the context of big data management, Microsoft has been able to define a price for data per unit, depending on its content and format. The data's impact value is not involved in Microsoft's development of the sale price. Only the costs of processing and structuring form the basis for this sales price.

These two examples taken from the SEA's cyberattacks highlight the great diversity of contexts that value data and finally the real difficulty in putting forward an absolute definition of the value of data. A systemic approach can contribute to prescribing the parameters and components that form the value of this data.

4.2.3. *Instantaneous value of interpreting data*

A systemic approach makes it possible to define the instantaneous value of interpreting data, in context, in relation to the algorithm that uses this data.

Data and binary words: a datum is represented by a finite set of binary words. A binary word is a finite binary sequence, that is, a finite sequence formed of 0s and 1s, interpretable by a calculation system. This definition makes it possible to bypass a datum's initial type (text, image, sound, video, signals or measurements from sensors). The total information contained in the initial data is translated into binary words according to a format compatible with future algorithmic processing.

Notations: a datum D is defined as a set by $D = \{ M_1, M_2,......, M_n \}$ where M_j are binary words such that $M_j = b_1b_2.....b_k$ and $b_i = 0$ or 1.

Vol(D) designates the volume expressed in bytes (or the size) of the non-compressed datum D. When the datum D is compressed with the help of a compression algorithm K, we write $Vol_K(D)$ the volume of the datum D after compression by K: $Vol_K(D) = Vol(K(D))$.

A program P taking D as input calculates the output P<D>. This program is run on a calculation system S.

Context, sub-context and system: a "context" will be used to designate a set of human, physical and algorithmic infrastructures linked to one another by relationships and data transfers ensuring a global systemic coherence. A context is formed of human users (operators) and physical and algorithmic systems ensuring interconnection. The context and its actors act depending on a set of economic and/or strategic goals. Any subset of a context is called a sub-context and can be considered as a more restricted context. For example, the international market for primary materials is a context, of which the market for cocoa is a sub-context. The art or energy markets are globalized contexts. A nation's defense and security infrastructure is a context at the national level. Silicon Valley, as a technical hub, is a local context, although it is highly globalized. A data center set up in Silicon Valley is therefore this context's sub-context.

We write a context as C, a physical and algorithmic system as S, considered to be a component of C, and as A an algorithm that can be run on the system S of the context C. A datum D will be valued in a context C, at an instant t, according to an algorithm A used to interpret it. The grouping of all the contexts is written Ω.

For any data D, the set Ω is expressed at the instant t in the form of a grouping:

$$\Omega = O_{D,t} \cup F_{D,t}$$

In this grouping, the component $O_{D,t}$ designates the grouping, at the instant t, of contexts with access to D's data content. The component $F_{D,t}$ designates the grouping, at the instant t, of contexts with no access to D's content. An instant indicator function is defined in the following way: $I_{C,t}(D) = 1$ if the context C has access to the data D at the instant t, otherwise $I_{C,t}(D) = 0$. Thus, $O_{D,t} = \cup$ C such that $I_{C,\,t}(D) = 1$ and $F_{D,t} = \cup$ C such that $I_{C,t}(D) = 0$.

A data is called public when it is known and accessible to all contexts, that is, if $O_{D,t} = \Omega$ and $F_{D,t}$ is empty. A data is called private at the instant t if $F_{D,t}$ is not void at instant t. In the course of time, private data can become public, but not vice versa. The set $O_{D,t}$ generally increases with time, in that the data set grows with time, whereas the set $F_{D,t}$ is never increasing with time since it is assumed that the data acquired is not lost over time.

4.2.3.1. *Instantaneous value of data in a context according to an algorithm*

If D is a datum accessible to the context C, and A an algorithm interpreting (operating) D, which can be run on the context's calculation system S, we will then write Val_t (D / C, A) the value at the instant t of D in relation to the context C and the algorithm A applied to D on C. The instantaneous digital value of Val_t (D / C, A) is a positive or a null value depending on the context and the operating algorithm. It corresponds to D's minimum potential price of sale by operators from the context C, at the instant t, after running algorithm A.

This time, using a program P implementing the algorithm A on a system, the interpretation value of a datum D by the program P relating to context C is a function which, at instant t, links Val_t (D / C, P). This value depends on the instant of evaluation t, on the program P taking D as input and calculating P<D>, and on the evaluation context C.

If the program P merely rewrites the data without modifying it, we then have: P<D> = D, and Val_t (D / C, P) = Val_t (D / C) which in this case designates the value of the raw data, which has not undergone processing.

If, on the contrary, P "refines" D by, for example, deleting the content noise, by deleting duplicates or by giving D a format pertinent for the context C, then running the program P brings value, compared to the raw data and we then have:

$$Val_t (D / C, P) > Val_t (D / C)$$

It is always actors and systems from the context C who evaluate and fix the datum's interpretation value. When the datum's veracity is established, its interpretation value increases. If P is a program certifying the datum's veracity, then when P confirms the veracity of D at instant t, we therefore have:

$$Val_t (D / C, P) > Val_t (D / C)$$

On the other hand, when P is not able to certify this veracity, Val_t (D / C, P) remains lower than or equal to the raw value Val_t (D / C). The datum may be true or false without the program P being able to detect it. The instantaneous interpretation value can then present strong gradients as shown in the emblematic example of the false Associated Press tweet and its impact on stock market indices in 2013.

4.2.3.2. Initial value of a datum in context

At the initial instant t = 0, the context C first becomes aware of the datum D's data content and uses it according to the A (which may only be a simple reading algorithm). This awareness of D's content may result from the production of D by a component of C that makes it public in C or from a simple purchase of data sold by C by a component from another context.

Val_0 (D / C, A) therefore designates the initial value of the datum D in C according to A. It may be equal to the sales price, by the context of the datum D, or even to its production cost if the context has produced this datum itself.

When a datum D is public, its instantaneous value cannot be null, and we therefore speak of the datum's residual value. A context can in fact have an interest in buying a set of public data structured beforehand by another context. The cost of structuring the public data generates its value in other contexts.

The nature of the interpretation algorithm A of the datum D in the context C directly influences its instantaneous value.

Let us suppose, for example, that A designates an algorithm that begins by reading the datum D and then calculates the probability p(D, t) that this datum is true at instant t. This program proceeds to a veracity test on the datum before it is used in a big data environment (big data technologies) or semantic analysis. If p(D,t) proves to be close to zero after calculation, the datum's value will also be close to zero in a rational context. If, on the contrary, this probability is close to 1, the context will consider the datum as true or nearly true (certified data) and can then attribute it an instantaneous value that will depend on the market and interactions between contexts.

When D, C and A are fixed, the function that, at instant t, matches Val_t (D /C,A) describes the instantaneous variations of the datum D's value in context C according to the interpretation algorithm A. This value changes over time, from an initial value Val_0 (D /C,A) corresponding to D's production cost in C or to its buying price at instant t = 0, up to its residual value written Val_∞(D /C,A). Such a function can present strong discontinuities as the example of the false tweet created by the SEA shows. It can on the other hand be constant in the context that has produced and structured it, as in the example of customer data sold legally by Microsoft to the FBI for 200 dollars per unit.

The instantaneous value directly depends on demand from contexts that still have no access to D and wish to buy it. Asymptotically, the more contexts there are that know the content of D, the more D's value approaches its residual value. When the data becomes public (that is, known to all contexts), the residual value is reached.

The example of the false SEA tweet: the data is the false tweet published on the AP agency account: D = {Explosion at the White House, President Obama is injured}

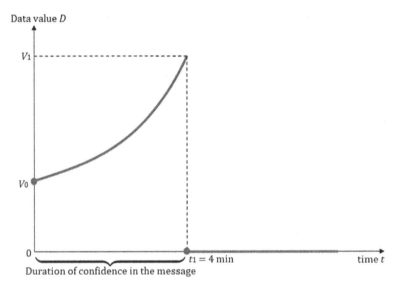

Figure 4.1. *The data value of the SEA tweet*

At instant t = 0, the SEA tweet is published on the AP agency account and remains accessible and credible for four minutes. At instant t_1 = 4, the AP agency and the White House publish a denial that immediately cancels the instantaneous value of the data D.

The quantity V_0 designates the data's production and insertion value on the AP account. This value takes account of the global cost of the SEA hijacking the account.

Quantity V_1 is the data's maximum value before AP regained control of the account. It can take into account the false tweet's impact value on the markets.

Figure 4.1 describes the data's instantaneous interpretation value produced by the SEA and shows this value's discontinuity once the denial had been published. The interpretation value grows exponentially from an initial value V0 to a maximum V1 and is then cancelled when AP retakes control of its account and reveals the attack. The raw data resulting from the cyberattack therefore has a high interpretation value during these four minutes and an even more substantial impact value, since it rose to more than 136 billion dollars on the stock markets.

It can be seen that a datum's impact value may be independent of its veracity. It is first and foremost the credit or confidence that a datum is given that its impact value can be based on. The example of the SEA's fake tweet illustrates the power and complexity of the interactions that exist and operate between the datum's value and veracity. It therefore shows all the benefits, for the interpretation context, of favoring certified data when the veracity of this data is "calculable" during the collection phase.

4.2.3.3. The instance of customer data sold legally by Microsoft to the FBI

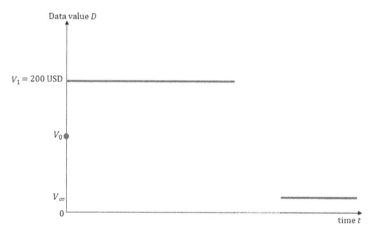

Figure 4.2. The value of data sold legally by Microsoft to the FBI

The instantaneous value of a set of customer data D sold by Microsoft to the FBI is constant over the validity period: Val_t (D / C, A) = 200 USD for t > 0 in the context of Microsoft production. A is a structuring (or formatting) and reading algorithm for the data. The quantity V_0 is the cost of structuring, formatting and storing the data for Microsoft. Quantity V_1 designates the unitary sales price by Microsoft to the FBI. Quantity V_∞ is the data's residual value.

Refining data: when D, C and t are fixed, we say that algorithm A' refines the data D in C at the instant t better than algorithm A if: $\mathrm{Val}_t (D / C, A') \geq \mathrm{Val}_t (D / C, A)$.

This is the case, for example, when A reads the data D in context, whereas A' reads this data, evaluates its veracity probability at instant t and shows that it is close to 1. The second algorithm provides confidence in the data and therefore increases its instantaneous value and refines this data in C, better than A, at instant t. On the contrary, if the probability calculated by A' is close to 0, then $\mathrm{Val}_t (D / C, A')$ will be close to 0 and will in this case be increased by $\mathrm{Val}_t (D / C, A)$ which does not take account of D's veracity.

Instantaneous value and sub-context: if C_1 is a sub-context of C_2, then for a fixed datum D, for a fixed algorithm A and a fixed instant t, it is not generally possible to compare $\mathrm{Val}_t (D / C_1, A)$ and $\mathrm{Val}_t (D / C_2, A)$. In fact, algorithm A can prove more effective for developing data in the sub-context or on the contrary in the broader context.

The data's origin and nature: when the data D is engendered in context C, it is said that C is its context of origin. This is the case when D is produced by a calculation system installed on C (connected objects, automated surveillance systems, measuring instruments). This origin gives it a systemic nature. The data can also be produced by a human operator, following an interaction with a calculation system. It is then an algorithmic projection by an operator, according to an algorithm run on a system from the context. In this case, the data is retrieved by an algorithmic projection $D = P_S (H/A)$. We then call it projective data. The global volume of systemic data is currently increasing very rapidly and exceeds that of projective data in some contexts. What will the consequence be for the value of this data? Will systemic data be valued less than projective data?

Data dissemination: the formalism that makes it possible to define a datum's instantaneous value can be completed by three effective measures for disseminating data in a context: the audience, the echo and the impact of a datum D.

The instantaneous audience of a datum D in a context C, written Aud_t (D/C), measures the fraction of the population of operators in the context C who have access to the datum D. This is a real number between 0 and 1, which amounts to 1 if any operator in the context has access to the data without any particular restriction and 0 if, on the contrary, no operator from the context has access to it. Open public data is by definition accessible to any operator who has an interconnected calculation system. Its audience is therefore equal to 1 in any context.

The instantaneous echo of datum D in a context C, written $Echo_t$ (D/C), measures the fraction of the population of operators from the context C who, having access to this data, really use it.

Finally, the instantaneous impact of a datum D in a context C, written Imp_t (D/C), measures the datum's effect in context, that is, its ability to change the state of the context, its parameters, its responses and definitively its entropy. The impact is certainly the most difficult quantity to discern and formally define according to the context's characteristics and its interconnection to other contexts. The data's global impact on the grouping of all the contexts determines its impact value. Similarly, the data's instantaneous audience and echo influence its instantaneous value. Are there therefore simple functional relationships between these three measures and a datum's instantaneous value? This question remains open.

A relative and functional approach (which is deliberately removed from any attempt at an absolute description of datum's value) seems adapted to the volatility and complexity of this value. If the instantaneous interpretation value really offers an individual approach to a datum's value, the big data context requires a global consideration. The big data set has a value based on the internal relationships linking these data, in their collective sense, and on the information resulting from this set. The gain obtained after operating the data set confers on it its global value.

4.3. The value of a body of big data

Megadata or big data are involved in all industrial, economic and social activities [DGC 13, HIG 10]. Its operation is profoundly altering our relationship with the world and providing fundamental tools that make it possible to remove uncertainty, and to understand and sometimes control complex phenomena. By transforming digital and physical spaces, the influx of data influences and directs economic, social and political practices. New scales of time and space are thus becoming accessible to human interpretation and understanding while still providing ever more technological challenges. Whether it is created by the individual or by connected infrastructure, data today provides an increasingly precise image of reality. The main challenge therefore lies in using this data and in our ability to benefit from a big data set to improve a process, build a forecast to organize an event, establish recommendations for products and services (forecasting), or even optimize aids for decision making [RAP 14, KEM 15]. Big data technologies go beyond simply making the data speak, they create meaning and produce effective solutions. This power for analyzing megadata naturally relies on the prerequisite of quality: a datum's veracity and value condition the entire process of using it. They are its basis and should be subject to systematic questioning.

4.3.1. *The qualities of a body of big data in 6V*

The Gartner firm and IBM use the six Vs fundamental for describing big data sets (or the big data domain): Volume, Variety, Velocity, Visibility, Value and Veracity.

The volume is linked to multiple data production sources [JAN 11a, BUL 13]. Whether this means business data, public data, data from transactions, data produced by automated sensors or objects connected or published on social media, this information is always collected and stored using digital supports in the form of binary files. Their volume is therefore easily calculable. Thus, the global production of data will in 2020 reach 40 Zo (one Zo is equal to 10^{21} bytes). This production's evolution is exponential: 90% of current data were produced in the last two years [MCK 11]. The emergence of connected cities and then ubiquitous cities reinforces this trend. By installing ubiquitous data – permanently accessible information available to everyone, everywhere – connected objects and geolocation contribute massively to the influx of data.

The variety results from heterogeneous data sources, which are often unstructured or barely structured (data from sensors, geolocation data, sound, videos, texts, etc.). This variety motivated the building of systems capable of "managing" the lack of structure (NoSql, Hadoop, etc.) while still ensuring a better distribution of the volume load on the calculation infrastructure. Like volume, variety is measured simply by counting the different formats present in the big data corpus to be processed. Algorithmic projections play a role in the variety of data.

Velocity is involved in moving data contexts, data streaming and processing this data in real time. It is linked to the source's production speed, to flux and to the system's flow and collection speed. Here again, velocity is an easily measurable quantity.

Data visibility strongly depends on the storage support, on the open (or otherwise) character of the information and the efficiency of collection algorithms and other crawlers.

These first four Vs could be completed by that of data variability in some contexts. This variability is expressed for data whose content evolves in time and space. These evolutions then produce new data indexed by time. The latter two Vs designate a datum's value and veracity. These qualities are much more complex to define and measure than the first four.

Veracity directly conditions the data's pertinence. Although uncertain data can be processed just as well as "certified" data, their interpretation in the context of false data can engender strong turbulence on all associated systems and trigger damaging consequences when decisions are taken on the basis of this interpretation.

4.3.2. Value of a big data corpus

We now place ourselves in a big data context and will define the value of a data set based on the gain obtained after this set is used by a calculation system.

In this section, D will designate a (voluminous) dataset $D = \{D_1, D_2,....,D_n\}$. This assumes that the set's cardinal (n) is high, high enough for the deletion of one or some data in the set not to influence the calculation result that uses this set. The set D can be run on a calculation system S grouping algorithms and machines.

Constraint line: for an organization (business, administration, institution, laboratory), a constraint line L designates a sub-domain of the organization's activity that directly influences its performance, efficiency and profitability. The constraint line can be temporal when it relates to the time needed for a production process or spatial when there is a distance or surface to be prospected. L can also involve a team in human resources (the number of engineers allocated to a project) or even the cost of developing an object or a service.

Value of a body of big data: a constraint line L is associated with its evaluation function $C_L(t)$, which depends on the instant t of measurement. The evaluation function can, for example, designate the cost of a process, its duration, or indeed a volume, surface or length, or even the team of personnel involved in this process. The gain obtained on the constraint line L after the data set D is operated by the calculation system S is written as:

$G_L(D, S) = C_L$(after D is operated by S) $- C_L$(before D is operated by S) $= \Delta C_L$

It is therefore possible to define the value $V_L(D)$ of the data set D on the constraint line L by considering the maximum gains obtained when the calculation system S, which processes D, is made to vary: $V_L(D) = k_L \max_S [G_L(D, S)]$.

Factor k_L is a constant depending on the constraint line L. It is a normalization coefficient defined for each constraint line. If several constraint lines are impacted by processing D, the factor k_L can also represent the weight given to L compared to the other constraint lines. It therefore makes it possible to create a hierarchy of constraint lines. We note that calculating the precise value of $V_L(D)$ would amount to rotating the calculation systems S on the data set D and then selecting the one (or ones) that produce the best gain on L. It is therefore an asymptotic definition of the value of a data set with which one might be content with an approximation approaching $V_L(D)$ using lower values.

We now give two concrete cases for which the value of a data set would be approached in the context of processing big data.

4.3.2.1. *The case of Vestas wind turbines*

The implementation of analysis carried out with the help of big data technologies has made it possible for Vestas to develop Vestas wind turbines to optimize its process of identifying the best locations to install the turbines. Big data processing has caused an increase in electricity generation performance and a reduction in the associated energy costs [IBM 11, IBM 12].

Thanks to meteorological big data, Vestas is able to describe the behavior of the wind in a chosen zone and provide an analysis of the precise profitability to its customers. The Vestas-IBM big data system has led to a 97% reduction in response times for wind forecasts from several weeks to only a few hours. The production cost per kilowatt-hour for customers has been reduced as well as the cost and data overload linked to a decrease of more than 40% in energy consumption. The meteorological database "Vestas wind turbine" reaches 24 petabytes. The IBM software infoSphere BigInsights running on an x-iDataPlex system has helped the Vestas group in managing meteorological and location data.

Processing this big data set has decreased the basic resolution of aerial data grids from a basic area of 27×27 kilometers to an area of 3×3 kilometers after calculations. In this megadata processing, the line of constraint L corresponds to the basic resolution of data grids, that is, a surface expressed in kilometers squared. The gain obtained from using data reduces spatial uncertainty by more than 90% and gives a precise (and almost immediate) overview of the best site for installing wind turbines in the zone studied.

$G_L(D, S) = -720$ km^2 which is a 98% gain in precision after processing and the value of the Vestas-turbine data set verifies $VL(D) > 720$ k_L.

4.3.2.2. *The case of Cincinnati zoo*

Facing profitability issues, the American zoo in Cincinnati (Ohio) turned to big data processing for its customer data and data from sensors used in the park's attractions and buildings [IBM 12]. The image in real time of customer behavior at the zoo made it possible to increase visitor expenditure by 25%, bringing in more than 350,000 dollars of additional spending per year.

A refined understanding of customer data has been applied to optimizing human resources at the zoo and has freed up time for personnel, who are now available for other, profitable posts. The business' budget thus has regained its equilibrium.

In this case, the constraint line L corresponds to annual income in dollars: $G_L(D, S) = 350,000$ USD which is a 25% annual gain and $V_L(D) > 350,000$ k_L.

Whether it is data of 140 characters or a corpus of several terabytes, the impact value of this set always remains highly "scalable" (a scalable quantity presents no visible upper limit and can move to very high scales). This value scalability, which exists independently of the data's veracity, can be the source of strong turbulence on the financial markets or on unstable economic or strategic balances. Moreover, it is used more and more regularly during cyberattacks (HoaxCrash) with the aim of influencing systems and operators. The question of the data's veracity overlays that of its value. This is the subject of the next chapter.

5

False Data and Fictitious Algorithmic Projections

5.1. Proliferation of fictitious data and fake profiles

5.1.1. *An influx of false data and bots as the majority of visitors*

The creation of false data (data conveying false information) can be considered as a collateral effect of the algorithmization of the environment. The use of false or fictitious data always responds to an initial aim to fool or dissimulate that can be expressed in very varied contexts, such as protecting anonymity, economic or military inquiries, cyber-espionage, cyber-crime, financial fraud or the manipulation of stock for listed companies. Creators of false data seek to deceive a number of users or a calculation system with the aim of benefitting from doing so.

All inquiries or studies highlight a substantial and regular increase in the volume of fictitious data or data of systemic origin imitating data created by human users. The large-scale use of robots (bots) contributes to raising the false data total. In 2013, more than 61% of traffic was generated by robots, with an increase of 21.5% between 2012 and 2013.

Bot traffic browsing web pages has not stopped growing since the early 2010s.

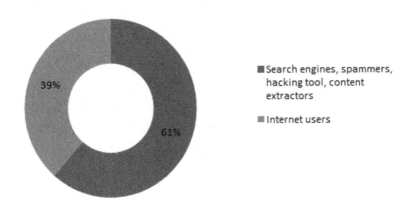

Figure 5.1. *Human/bot distribution of website visitors (2013–2014).*
For a color version of this figure, see www.iste.co.uk/berthier/digital.zip

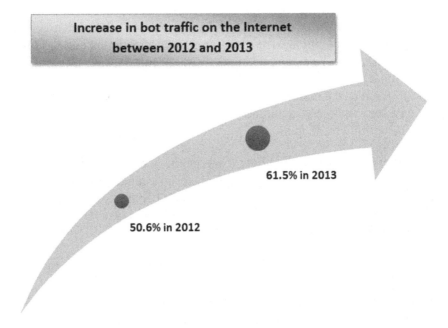

Figure 5.2. *Increase in bot traffic on the Internet between 2012 and 2013*

5.1.2. *False data for protecting anonymity*

According to a report addressing the protection of private data published in 2015 by the cybersecurity firm Symantec, 57% of Europeans worry about the security of their personal data, 81% believe that their data are worth more than a thousand euros and 31% no longer hesitate to communicate with false data systems to protect their personal data. Applications have been developed to create false data with the aim of fooling Android applications that users sometimes feel are too intrusive. XPrivacy is a tool that makes it possible to supply Android applications with false contacts, false geographical coordinates, false user dictionaries, false clipboards, false call histories and false SMSs. The aim advertised by XPrivacy is to create false data in order to better manage a customer's private life. In the same vein, the site FakeNameGenerator makes it possible to build a database in various formats (MS SQL, MySQL, IBM DB2, Oracle, etc.) of 50,000 coherent fictitious identities, including name, age, nationality, address and profession for the registered profiles. The CloneZone site immediately clones any website and suggests modifying or distorting all or part of its content.

5.1.3. *Toward proliferation of fictitious profiles on social networks*

The success of social networks is characterized by a regular increase in the number of user profiles. Nevertheless, the number of fictitious profiles, fake profiles or profiles resulting from identity theft has never been as high as it is now. This trend, which is seen across all platforms, should make us query the confidence that can be accorded a body of data forming a profile. This user profile appears first as a changing set of voluntary and systemic algorithmic projections.

To counter this regular increase in fake profiles, Facebook has a moderator service and a set of algorithmic tools dedicated to detecting the inconsistencies and weak signals that characterize these fictitious data. It will be noted that, given the volumes of data to be processed, detection can only result from a scalable algorithmic platform (capable of scaling) relying on automated learning. Figure 5.4 shows the number of profiles belonging to the main social networks in July 2017. An average rate of 10% for fake profiles thus represents tens of millions of fictitious profiles to detect and then deactivate. This cleanup work (detection/deletion) therefore appears to be a colossal challenge for the group administrators in charge of large social networks!

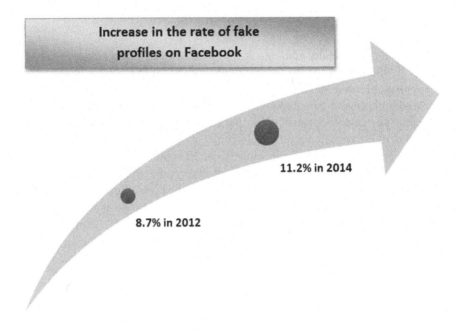

Figure 5.3. *Increase in fake profiles on Facebook between 2005 and 2014 (source: Facebook)*

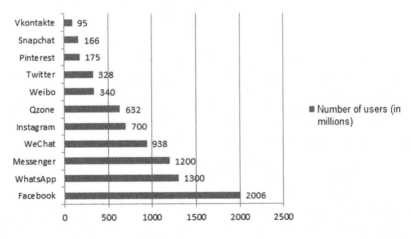

Figure 5.4. *Number of profiles registered on the main social networks (source: data provided by businesses from December 2016 to July 2017)*

The Twitter network had nearly 8.5% fake profiles active in 2014, according to a low estimation made by the group's directors. On Instagram, administrators estimated a figure of 10% for fake profiles in 2014–2015.

In general, it is simple to create a fake profile on a social network. It can be done by a robot that generates fictitious profiles or by a human actor stealing the identity of another individual. The conditions of use for large social networks try to protect them from this proliferation of fake profiles from the signing up process. Thus, on Facebook, the new user must agree to declarations of good conduct of the kind "You will not provide any false personal information on Facebook or create an account for anyone other than yourself without permission". These conditions of use for the social network barely engage the signatory who can then proceed as he/she wishes. While Instagram forbids the creation of accounts for other people, Twitter specifies less abruptly that: "When circumstances justify it, Twitter will have the right to terminate a user's account if it has been considered on several occasions to be fraudulent". To guarantee the veracity of some high-level profiles, Twitter has implemented a blue verified badge. This device is reserved for the time being for much searched users in the fields of music, the performance industry, fashion, the government, politics, religion, journalism, the media, high-level sport, business and other major centers of interest.

Legally, it is still rare for an Internet user who generates fictitious profiles to be convicted. However, some cases have been reported, especially that of a jealous husband who recreated a fictitious Facebook account for his former wife with the aim of discrediting her (in 2011). Another case (in 2010) involved the identity theft of a French comedian (Omar Sy) via a fake Facebook account. The thief was convicted for invasion of privacy and the French right to one's image.

5.1.4. Purchasing fake subscribers to build popularity

In 2015, the social network Instagram had begun to "clean up" all the accounts marked as fictitious, dubious or inactive. Suspending these accounts almost instantly shed millions of followers for stars in the music industry and in politics. This digital purge revealed the scale of the practice of buying fictitious fans on social networks with the aim of boosting an artistic career or artificially boosting burgeoning popularity. It is in fact very easy to buy lots fans on the Internet and use them to increase the number of views for a video posted on YouTube or to reinforce a Facebook or Twitter profile. Prices vary from a few euros for a few hundred fans to several thousand euros for a million or more subscribers. The sites that provide this type of service may rely on two often complementary strategies: they create lots of fictitious profiles via more or less sophisticated algorithmic robots and then complete this fictitious lot with lots of real Internet users, voluntary and remunerated to become "followers" of the customer's page or video. This commercial practice is still legal and often very lucrative. The French site "acheter-des-fans.com", active since 2011, claims that more than 3,000 customers are satisfied with the quality of service. This platform declares that it relies only on the profiles of real Internet users based in France. They are paid using online presents or micro-payments, participation in competitions or free access to paying content. Other firms go through sub-contractors situated in Asia, India or Pakistan which offer large-scale lots for low prices. All the actors involved in buying fictitious profiles seem to benefit in this dubious practice, which still generates an illusion of online popularity! Who buys lots of followers? Sites selling profiles say that their customers are extremely diverse: commercial centers, big brands, community managers, communications agencies, publicity agencies, agents for sports stars or political personalities, local or national representatives before an election and new artists wanting to negotiate their first contract with a producer. The list of customers is as long as it is varied. It involves all pursuits that rely partially or entirely on popularity (real and digital) as a factor.

Table 5.1 provides information on the prices for different batches of fans and followers in France in 2017.

For political personalities, the large-scale purchasing of followers for a third party often relates to an operation using manipulation that can then influence the positioning of part of the electorate. It will be noted that it is still difficult to precisely measure the electoral impact of buying a million fictitious followers for a candidate's Twitter and/or Facebook account.

	Batch of 100 profiles	Batch of 1,000 profiles	Large lots of profiles
French Facebook fans	15 euros	129 euros	Batch of 15,000 profiles: 1,299 euros
International Facebook fans	5 euros	28 euros	Batch of 100,000 profiles: 999 euros
French Twitter followers	29 euros	199 euros	Batch of 5,000 followers: 649 euros
French Instagram followers	39 euros	349 euros	Batch of 25,000 followers: 4,999 euros
International Instagram followers	5 euros	19 euros	Batch of 1,000,000 followers: 4,999 euros
Buying views on YouTube	–	5 euros for 1,000 views	1,890 euros for 1,000,000 views
International YouTube subscribers	29 euros	169 euros	999 euros for 10,000 subscribers
Buying a Google review (French or international)	19 euros or a Google review	–	–
Buying five-star reviews for a Facebook page	99 euros for 100 notes	899 euros for 1,000 notes	–

Table 5.1. *French prices in 2017 for batches of fans and followers*

Although the conditions of use for the main social networks actually forbid the purchase of fake notoriety on the Internet, the law does not forbid this practice, which can still fool advertisers in publicity contracts. Since 2015, Facebook and Twitter have put in place algorithmic tools for detecting and deleting fictitious or inactive accounts. Specialist sites such as Socialbakers, Twitter Audit and StatusPeople say they are able to evaluate the percentage of false subscribers to a Twitter account. Nevertheless, detecting fake profiles is still a complex algorithmic operation that can produce a large number of "false positives", i.e. inactive or barely active but legitimate profiles (on Twitter, 40% of subscribers do not tweet regularly!).

5.1.5. *The specific case of Twitter*

Created in 2006, the social network Twitter detected its first fictitious profile in 2007 (January 2007, compte @krails) and then put in place the first account verification in June 2009 and account authentication in August 2010. An analysis of the accounts of personalities known in the world of drama and politics in 2012 reported rates of fake profiles sometimes exceeding 30%, as shown in Table 5.2.

Twitter accounts	Total number of followers in August 2012	Percentage of fake profiles	Percentage of inactive profiles	Real active profiles
Lady Gaga @ladygaga	28,839,110	34%	38%	28% 8,074,950
Justin Bieber @justinbieber	27,176,769	31%	40%	29% 7,881,263
Katy Perry @katyperry	25,678,355	32%	42%	26% 6,676,372
Britney Spears @britneyspears	19,830,606	33%	41%	26% 5,155,957
Barack Obama @barackobama	18,964,766	29%	38%	33% 6,258,372
YouTube @youtube	15,688,501	27%	42%	31% 4,863,435
Twitter @twitter	12,837,573	37%	40%	23% 2,952,641
CNN Breaking @cnnbrk	8,585,934	30%	43%	27% 2,318,202
ESPN @espn	5,112,022	32%	41%	27% 1,380,245
Facebook @facebook	4,500,928	39%	42%	19% 855,176
Google @google	5,220,100	31%	40%	29% 1,513,829
Instagram @instagram	8,372,543	15%	28%	57% 4,772,349

Table 5.2. *Source: www.statuspeople – August 2012*

The Twitter accounts of political figures have also not escaped the temptation to artificially increase notoriety. The account of Mitt Romney, an American politician, registered a 17% increase in less than 24 h between 20 and 21 July 2012, from 673,002 followers to 789,924 followers. More than 80% of these accounts had been created less than 3 months prior and 25% of them had never produced a single tweet.

5.1.5.1. Influence operations, fake profiles and social bots

Social networks are regularly used by institutions and political parties in their communication strategies. Official accounts on Twitter and Facebook have been incorporated into electoral campaigns, for better or worse, especially when hacking operations come to disrupt them. Armed groups, rebels or terrorists also know how to use them to spread their propaganda or to recruit future combatants.

At the heart of influence operations, fictitious profiles and bots play a significant role in duplicating and directing information. Thus, between 2015–2016, only 35% of the 500 million Twitter accounts would actually be managed by a human user. These fake profiles are shared between copies of legitimate profiles and fictitious profiles formed from elements of real aggregated profiles and influence data. Fake profiles are mainly created and supervised by social bots, automated programs or software robots that imitate, with greater or lesser success, the behavior of real profiles. Everything depends in fact on the level of artificial intelligence that drives the bot. Although no bot today can formally pass the Turing test successfully, some of them are still able to fool a large number of users who do not always detect the automated nature of the tweets that they produce. The most sophisticated bots use text mining techniques, NLP (natural language processing) and semantic analysis to imitate, under good conditions, human conversations. They may have access to general knowledge databases and databases of events, which they grow in order to recognize other interlocutors' references and then are able to produce adapted and pertinent responses.

There are thus five main families of social bots, identified in a study by the group Diplomatie-Digitale and CEIS dating from 2016:

The family of relay social bots: rudimentary bots in this category react to simple keywords, hashtags or specific groups of words. They are built to systematically "retweet" or "favorite" certain tweets and act to repeat them.

Easily detectable and imbued with very little AI, they cannot be confused with profiles of human operators.

The family of provider social bots: provider bots act like relay bots but with more power and reliability. The AI level they are imbued with is more substantial, which gives them a broader perimeter of action. They are used to carry out directed overviews of a body of hashtags, expressions or keywords. They then provide pertinent data in exchanges.

The family of spammer social bots: these are the most rudimentary bots in terms of features. They are responsible for spreading, en masse and in distributed fashion, specific, predefined information. They are generally very efficient at providing a strong echo for information that the operators wish to highlight quickly on Twitter.

The family of follower social bots: this family of bots could represent more than 45% of accounts that follow business accounts on Twitter. Their role is to follow a particular account whose supervisor has purchased followers to increase their notoriety. The follower account retweets some publications by the source account. Its detection is simple, since retweet content without producing original messages.

The family of complex influencer social bots: this family designates bots with a high-level of sophistication. They are capable of acquiring notoriety independently. Thanks to their level of AI, they can exchange messages with human profiles and remain difficult to detect among legitimate profiles who express themselves badly. The influencer social bot is the most complex bot to use. This can also have the most effect in an organized disinformation campaign.

5.1.5.2. *Detecting fake profiles on Twitter*

From 2011, studies have been published for detecting social bots on Twitter. The developed techniques are often complementary [TEC 14].

The first technique was derived from research by a team from the University of Texas (Texas A&M University). They relied on creating a "honeypot" (digital bait) that can only be detected by social bots. The tweets used for the honeypot have no meaning for a human user but are very "communicative" for a robot. The research team began by creating 60 "honeypot" tweets whose content was absurd and lacked interest for a human reader but not for the bots, since more than 30,000 Twitter accounts have reacted to these baits by retweeting them or adding them as favorite tweets. These 30,000 accounts have been analyzed and the study has shown that the vast majority are relay or provider social bots. Nevertheless, new, influencer social bots imbued with AI cannot be detected by this first method.

A research team from the University of Indiana in Bloomington focused on detecting social bots endowed with effective AI. For this, they used 35,000 Twitter accounts detected by the first team in 2011, via honeypot, of which 15,000 have been studied by analyzing the last 200 tweets by these accounts and the 100 most recent tweets referring to the first 200 tweets. A database was thus built, containing more than 2.6 million reference tweets. The same operation was carried out with a panel of 16,000 human users producing 3 million reference tweets.

The two databases built were then compared via the "Bot or Not" algorithm [OSO 18]. Bot or Not measured significant differences between the tweets produced by human users and those produced by bots. The measurements relied on more than 1,000 parameters and characteristics linked to the accounts analyzed, including the number of tweets and retweets, the number of exchanges, responses, the account user name, the length, date of creation and its duration. This fine big data analysis has revealed characteristic "patterns" on accounts held by bots:

– social bots have a retweet rate much higher than human accounts;

– the length of a social bot's user name is longer on average than that of human accounts; and

– human accounts have a higher response rate than bot accounts; they are also, on average, mentioned more often in accounts of other users.

These patterns have made it possible to draw up a "robot portrait" of rudimentary social bots.

It will be noted that the former limitation on the length of tweets to 140 characters favors the possibility of imitation by a social bot. Beyond 140 characters, it is much more difficult for a robot to maintain coherent and general exchanges. We recall that at the end of 2017, no public chat bot system has successfully passed the Turing test!

The creation and supervision of fictitious accounts managed by a social bot is more complex on Facebook than on Twitter. Detection of false accounts on Facebook can be fast when it involves fictitious accounts built from elements taken from legitimate accounts.

As for photos, the reverse image search is a function offered by Google, which often makes it possible to detect the origin of stolen, "borrowed" data. Analyzing friends on a Facebook account, their number and relationship can also serve as a warning. Finally, in the manner of the Turing test, it is possible, if in doubt, to post a list of questions whose answers might characterize the fake account.

5.1.5.3. Influence of social bots

In 2011, the "Carina Santos" experiment [MES 13], carried out by a team of researchers from the Federal University of Ouro Preto, showed that it is possible to build a fictitious profile that rapidly gains a high level of influence, according to measurements put in place by Twitter. The fictitious bot account of the journalist Carina Santos (@Scarina91) was built to be as credible as possible. It ceased following accounts that did not follow it after 4 days. The content posted by Carina came from real information linked to world news. The social bot copied some tweets and retweeted others while avoiding any mechanical or periodic behavior. The rhythm of publication was kept up randomly.

After some weeks of activity, influence measurements made using the analysis tool Twitalyzer showed that the Carina Santos account's level of influence exceeded that of the legitimate account of Oprah Winfrey, a famous American presenter.

Finally, the operation "The Dawn of Glad Tidings", carried out by Islamic State in 2014, showed its perfect mastery of influence mechanisms adapted to social networks. The application designed by IS could be downloaded from the Google Play Store. Once installed, it was able to take control of a Twitter account or tweet in place of the legitimate user. Thus, on a single day, 10 June 2014, which marked the taking of Mosul by IS, more than 40,000 tweets were made in less than 2 h by users who had installed the application. The act of taking control of Twitter accounts by an influence social bot therefore serves very directly as propaganda for a terrorist group.

5.1.6. *The Tinder networking application and its derivatives*

Launched in 2012, the social networking application Tinder acts as a site for making contact and meeting online. It puts users in contact with one another according to affinities established from looking at profiles (photos and a description of the users' interests). The principle behind its function is simple: the application scrolls through user profiles according to different criteria, including geographical position and gender. The user should therefore sort each profile suggested by indicating if they like them or if they "scrap" them by "swiping", i.e. by swiping the screen to the left or right. If there is reciprocal interest between two profiles, the application puts them in contact.

The Tinder application, which is not sufficiently secure, has been subject to several cyber-attacks. In March 2015, a hacker exploited a security failing enabling him to link heterosexual men to one another, by constructing fictitious female profiles. Other attacks relying on vulnerabilities native to the application and on creating fake profiles triggered a high-level of disruption in Tinder's functioning.

The example of the English model, Matt Peacock, speaks for itself. His photo was stolen and used in 43 different Tinder profiles. Male users recovered public photos of Matt Peacock to create a profile that was attractive in the eyes of female users and could then entrap them. Matt Peacock employed a detective to identify the 43 individuals stealing his identity and forced them to close their Tinder accounts. The aim of these fraudsters was to attract female profiles and extract personal photos from them after establishing a relationship characterized by seduction and confidence. Once these photos were obtained, some thieves were able to blackmail, threatening victims that they would make the photos public. One of the women tricked said she considered suicide after this digital ambush. Matt Peacock's wife and family had a very unpleasant experience with these identity thefts. It was not possible to file a complaint against the fraudsters since nothing in British law foresaw this type of digital attack. The profiles were created around his photo, but from a legal point of view, their content did not steal Matt Peacock's legitimate profile. In view of the human suffering caused by this type of fraud, it now seems that this legal loophole urgently needs filling in.

It is conceivable that the process of detecting fake profiles on Tinder could be automated, since there is often a "shared pattern" used when they are created by a bot or a single individual. Among the motivations for creators of fake profiles, we find blackmail, the wish to lead targets to certain paying or surcharged services or even the desire to induce them to download malicious applications on smartphones. Once created, the fictitious profiles, always very attractive, often interact in similar ways: they begin by "liking" all the male profiles who introduce themselves, then start a conversation by adapting the fake profile's interests to those of their quarry. Sometimes, it is a seduction game enacted in front of a webcam (booty cam) recording all their interactions. This video then serves as a tool for blackmail to extort several thousand euros from the victim of the impersonation game, by threatening to put the video online and send it to all the contacts in their email account! In this matter, the blackmailers' malicious imaginations are limitless. On Tinder, these fictitious profiles often show three low-quality teaser photos of a young woman with an American-sounding first name. The email header for these profiles is often the same, which makes automatic detection possible using machine learning techniques.

5.1.7. The "Robin Sage" experiment

In 2010 (Black Hat Conference 2010, Las Vegas), Thomas Ryan, a cybersecurity researcher, carried out an (already well-known) experiment, on a large scale, on the creation and use of a fictitious profile with the aim of establishing relationships with high-ranking personalities and then collecting sensitive information. The researcher, whose aim was to insert himself rapidly into networks of digital security experts, therefore began by creating an attractive fictitious profile, belonging to Robin Sage [RYA 10].

Robin Sage is a young woman of 25. She pursued her higher education at the prestigious MIT (Massachusetts Institute of Technology). She has had very promising professional experience and says she is a researcher in cybersecurity. Her profile photo belongs to a very beautiful young woman. Robin Sage's fictitious profile therefore relies on intelligence, youth and beauty to attract her future prey.

In only 28 days, more than 300 people were accepted as "friends" with Robin Sage on Facebook, Twitter and LinkedIn. Tens of experts and specialists from the worlds of digital security, intelligence and the military accepted invitations and added her to their respective networks on the three main social networks. More worryingly, some of these newly created relationships also gave her access to private data. Others, very impressed by the young researcher's record and global algorithmic projection, gave her job offers.

Among the American profiles entrapped were members of the Defense Department, the NSA, personnel in the American army, employees and executives of armament companies (Lockheed Martin and Northrop Grumman), as well as engineers and employees of large American digital companies including Google. It should be noted that no member of the FBI or the CIA fell into the trap. By using his fictitious profile, Thomas Ryan was able to gain access to one of the targets' email and bank account. He was able to guess answers to secret questions linked to the process of identifying two accounts, using the personal information collected from this target's profile (on their open algorithmic projection).

Through conversations with an American soldier on a mission to Afghanistan, Thomas Ryan obtained precise information on the takeoff times of military helicopters. Robin Sage's profile received several invitations to speak at cybersecurity conferences, invitations to lunch and gifts. The gifts were related more to the quality of the young woman's profile photo than to her academic education. The choice of this photo had considerable impact on the fictitious profile's success with men!

Sensitive data leaks on Facebook occurred the same year, this time involving a talkative Israeli soldier who revealed the existence of a military operation under preparation and which had to be canceled at the last minute following these leaks.

The "Robin Sage" experiment was particularly revealing about the level of human vulnerability faced with the digital cunning and deception used during a social engineering operation. It highlighted the full power of the cognitive biases that push us to be credulous and naive in some situations as long as the context is prepared beforehand by the attacker. Above all, it served as a warning about the ease of fooling high-level targets and collecting sensitive information while still deploying a rudimentary, fictitious digital device. According to Thomas Ryan, "The greatest lesson from the Robin Sage experiment was to not accept friend requests or make contacts without knowing who they really come from".

On Facebook, an Internet user brought to life the fictitious profile of "Mademoiselle Framboise Bertrand" for more than 6 years (2,370 days) before revealing the deceit in July 2017. Framboise Bertrand's Facebook account was at the time followed by more than 2,500 people. Treated as a game at the start, the management of this fictitious profile became, over time, a real immersion in a subtle exercise in imagining a coherent ecosystem around an individual. Framboise was designed as a naive, rebellious fighter who was waiting for her prince charming and her fifteen minutes of fame while still faced with small worries of daily life. After closing Framboise Bertrand's Facebook account, its supervisor converted the digital experiment into a book describing the fictitious life of this virtual young woman.

5.2. Projective representation of fictitious data

The formalism of algorithmic projections makes it possible to represent different cases of identity theft and the production of fictitious profiles. Two situations should be considered.

The first situation involves imitating the algorithmic projections of a real individual, active in the real world, with a more or less substantial legitimate global algorithmic projection. This is the typical context of identity theft, forbidden by the law.

The second situation involves creating a fictitious individual's fictitious algorithmic projections. The author of these fictitious projections (who may be an individual or a Bot) may use fragments of real projections (photos, videos, sounds, texts) to give body to their fictitious persona (there is therefore a partial identity theft), or, on the contrary, may limit themselves to projections without any link with real individuals. In the latter case, there is no theft in the legal sense of the term but only the deception associated with the physical non-existence of the simulated profile.

5.2.1. *The context of identity theft and the imitation of a real individual*

5.2.1.1. *A case of identity theft of collecting after collecting a real user's identifiers on a system S*

This context involves an individual H' who has obtained the identifiers and password of legitimate individual H on a system S. H' verifies their identity normally on S so that they pass for H.

Note therefore that P_S (H' --> H/A) the algorithmic projection created by H' on S, imitating H on S according to the algorithm A run on S. The arrow --> means "imitate" or "simulate". In this case, H' runs A on S as H would have been able to do legitimately. For an external observer, it is very difficult to detect identity theft since the projection is produced legitimately, after authenticating H' on S. By producing P_S (H' --> H/A), the individual H' seeks to imitate as well as possible the potential, legitimate algorithmic projection P_S (H/A).

5.2.1.2. *A case of identity theft from a real user, using imitation without identification on a system S*

In this context, the individual H' does not have H's identifiers on S. They are content to run an algorithm B on S imitating the running of A on S by H. The resulting projection is then written P_S (H'/B --> H/A). It designates the algorithmic projection of an individual H' running the algorithm B on S to imitate an individual H running the algorithm A on S.

By producing P_S (H'/B --> H/A), the individual H' seeks to simulate as well as possible the potential legitimate projection P_S (H/A) on the system S.

5.2.1.3. *A case of the identity theft of a real user from another system*

It is assumed in this case that the individual H' runs an algorithm B on a system S', different from S, to imitate individual H running A on S. We write the corresponding algorithmic projection $P_{S'-->S}$ (H'/B --> H/A). By producing $P_{S'-->S}$ (H'/B --> H/A), the individual H' seeks to simulate the potential legitimate projection P_S (H/A) on the system S as well as possible from the system S'.

These three cases of identity theft from a real user by another individual may be extended to a situation where the "thieving" individual H is replaced by a "robot" program (a Bot) activated on a system (S or S'). Social networks offer activation spaces particularly well-adapted to this type of robot thief. In the "Bot" context, we will keep the notations with:

P_S (Bot --> H/A): the algorithmic projection created by a Bot on S, imitating H on S according to algorithm A run on S. By running A on S, the Bot simulates the potential legitimate projection P_S (H/A).

P_S (Bot / B --> H/A): the algorithmic projection of a Bot running algorithm B on S to imitate an individual H running algorithm A on S. By running B on S, the Bot simulates the potential legitimate projection P_S (H/A).

$P_{S'->S}$ (Bot / B --> H/A): the algorithmic projection of a Bot running algorithm B on a system S' to imitate an individual H running algorithm A on S.

It will be noted that prior activation of the Bot on S by a user H has given rise to other algorithmic projections.

5.2.2. *Context for the creation of fictitious profiles*

It is no longer a question here of imitating or simulating the projections of an individual H who exists in "real life" but of building credible algorithmic projections corresponding to a fictitious person to give them a digital existence. Often, this construction is made from fragments of legitimate algorithmic projections "borrowed" from the Internet. The identity theft is therefore only partial and it is generally very difficult for victims to obtain reparation from the courts.

The main challenge for the creator-supervisor of fictitious profiles lies in maintaining an overall coherence of the different simulated algorithmic projections, i.e. all the fictitious projections P_S (.. --> H_{fic} /A) forming the digital imprint of a fictitious individual written H_{fic}.

Concretely, the supervisor (an individual H' or a Bot) should take care not to introduce contradictions or incoherences in the body of simulated projections. The more voluminous this corpus is in digital space and time, the more the risk increases of involuntarily introducing a contradiction that may then reveal the fictitious character of the whole digital construction.

Keeping a single fictitious profile active requires in particular continuous monitoring to ensure that the history of the simulated projections is not contradictory.

When it involves a group formed of several fictitious profiles interacting with one another and those outside the group, maintaining the construction's coherence quickly becomes critical in space and time. Ensuring that the whole is not self-contradictory requires numerous controls. The complexity can thus quickly become exponential with the membership and level of the group of fictitious profiles supervised.

5.2.2.1. *The complexity of keeping a group of fictitious profiles in coherence*

Let us imagine that we wish to construct a group formed of n fictitious profiles interacting internally and externally. The profiles created should be present on social networks and the usual large digital platforms. We write this fictitious set G_{fic}.

$$G_{fic} = \{ H^1_{fic} , H^2_{fic} , ... , H^n_{fic} \}$$

Any fictitious profile H^i_{fic} is represented at instant t by its global fictitious algorithmic projection $P(H^i_{fic}) = U_{S, A} P_S (H^i_{fic} /A)$. The fictitious projections forming this global projection should not contradict each other. Then, any subset extracted from $P(H^i_{fic})$ should not contradict any subset of fictitious projections resulting from $P(H^j_{fic})$.

As soon as the membership n increases, the probability of introducing a contradiction revealing the fictitious character of G_{fic} tends toward 1. In practice, a human operator wanting to build and supervise a group of 20 fictitious profiles, active on social networks and large digital platforms, should carry out several tens of coherence controls each time a new fictitious projection is added.

5.2.2.2. *Data confidence*

Whether "small data" or big data, it is really the confidence that is given to them that conditions their use. Just like its value, a datum's veracity depends on both the instant and context of its evaluation. In absolute terms, one must be able to go back, systematically, to the initial sender (the source) of a datum to ensure its integrity and conformity. This certification step, which is algorithmically costly, in fact, only involves the domain of sensitive data. On the contrary, one should not exclude failure of the certification process caused by an undetected hacking operation.

An initial approach consists of evaluating a datum's probability of veracity, given its sender, its reputation and history.

Probability (D true / Sender, Reputation, History),

As a second approach, for high-impact data, we should evaluate this probability considering the eventuality of a cyber-attack on D, which is:

Probability (D true / Sender, Reputation, History, *Proba*(Hacking(D)) > 0).

This expresses the confidence one has in D.

5.2.2.3. *System anti-fragility*

Experts in data science are already faced with new challenges, both complex and strategic. One of them involves detecting bodies of fictitious data and authenticating legitimate data.

The expertise of data quality specialists will be developed by growing cybersecurity competencies and data sciences.

The data quality specialist relies on algorithmic architectures capable of evaluating in real time the legitimacy of a data warning when false digital data have been detected.

In general, systems should evolve to become more resilient in the face of cyber-attacks. Anti-fragility [TAL 12], a concept introduced by Nassim Nicholas Taleb in 2012, can provide an efficient response to the proliferation of fictitious data. Going beyond the simplest notions of resistance and resilience, anti-fragility implies a regular improvement in the system in the wake of shocks undergone and a capacity to capitalize on random events to strengthen oneself. In the digital world, anti-fragility can only be installed following a rise in the power of the level of artificial intelligence mounted on the system. Finally, the data quality remains subordinate to the anti-fragility of the system processing it.

5.3. Fictitious algorithmic projections and cybersecurity

The production of coherent fictitious data sets is involved more and more often during the social engineering phase of preparing a cyber-attack. The human factor represents the first fragility exploited during a digital attack, well before system fragility. The main challenge for the attacker is creating room for confidence between them and their victim and then exploiting this confidence to carry out the attack successfully [BER 14]. The "energy" to be expended to instill confidence increases regularly with users' sensitization to digital risks and dangers. Nevertheless, several examples of sophisticated attacks relying on fictitious data structures have shown that the *initial* confidence accorded an attractive set of fictitious data that can induce vulnerability, including among victims very well informed about digital risks. This vulnerability of confidence given too easily is clearly a human factor and a factor of the attendant human cognitive bias that "pushes us to commit error".

5.3.1. *Economic interference from fake profiles*

Professional social networks such as LinkedIn and Viadeo are a favorite hunting ground for malicious actors looking for economic, technological or strategic information. Arising from economic intelligence methods, their practices rely on creating and broadcasting credible fake profiles, from which they will forge links with targets with high data value. These fake profiles can present themselves as recruitment professionals or headhunters working for a specialist office that is fictitious or whose identity has been stolen. They can also take on the appearance of a human resources manager or a senior executive in a large international group, regardless of their activity sector. Fictitious profiles are built in a very detailed way, often by integrating information from legitimate accounts and completed with a photo of a young man or woman taken from the Internet, which is generally easy to find. These fictitious accounts often display a large number of contacts or relationships, thus confirming their attractiveness.

The creator-supervisor of fictitious profiles, who we will call the attacker from now on, most often works from abroad. Their objective lies in making contact with personnel working in businesses already chosen as targets. Employees in this business receive requests to link with professionals on social networks. When the invitation has been accepted, the attacker can map precisely the targeted user's circles of professional relationships and can then obtain information for operational ends (location, hierarchical position in society, centers of interest, telephone number, email addresses, etc.).

Once confidence has been established between the attacker and their targets, the attacker will be able to exploit the information collected and then carry out cyber-attacks (identity theft, phishing, spear-phishing, sending an attachment containing malware, etc.). In all cases, the operational mode relies on a social engineering campaign, more or less sophisticated depending on the target's level of mistrust and security. A contact request sent from a fictitious profile should be considered as a weak signal announcing a subsequent attempted cyber-attack (intrusion into a business's information system, data theft, implanting malware, CryptoLocker ransomware) or a malicious approach.

In France, the National Cybersecurity Agency and General Directorate for Internal Security have published common sense recommendations to apply to any contact request on a professional social network. When this request comes from an unknown or suspect profile, the DGSI recommends:

– maintaining a high level of vigilance when contact requests come from unknown profiles;

– checking if the profile photo is a simple cut-and-pasted photo taken from the Internet (this verification can be carried out using Google Images or TinEye reverse image searches);

– checking if the profile description is plagiarized from the description of a legitimate profile by asking a search engine (Google is very good at recognizing copy-and-paste); and

– verifying the actual existence of the person described by the profile by cross-checking information from Google queries on the surname, first name and business figuring in the profile description and then checking the coherence of the dubious profile's academic and professional experience (dates, roles held, cities visited, etc.).

In case of doubt, the DGSI advises deleting the contact from one's personal network and remaining vigilant about unusual emails.

5.3.2. *A cyber-attack targeting a large consulting firm from a fictitious profile*

A famous consulting and auditing firm was the victim of a cyber-attack that was as substantial in its scope as its duration. Between the end of October 2016 and March 2017, a group of attackers gained access to the sensitive data of a large number of clients and, more precisely, to all the emails exchanged between the group's 244,000 employees and its clients! More than 5 million emails were affected. The start of this attack (its effects on the firm's image and confidence have still not been properly measured) relied on a fictitious profile to ensnare an employee of the group and then obtain privileged access to servers and the advisory firm's cloud service.

The fictitious individual used was a young woman, "Mia Ash", who had a Facebook page with several friends and relationships. The cybersecurity firm SecureWorks studied this fictitious profile and seems to attribute its creation and supervision to a group of Iranian hackers (OilRig) who may have benefitted from the support of the Iranian regime.

Mia forged close links with an employee and was able to develop a friendship that quickly bore fruit for the attacker. Once trust was established, Mia exchanged files, at first innocuous ones, with her new friend and then sent him a file corrupted by malware, which was installed on his machine. This malicious software then exfiltrated the employee's identifiers to the attacker, thus giving them privileged administrator access to part of the advisory firm's IT system.

This scenario, effective for the attacker and arising from economic warfare, thus became the norm in similar operations penetrating large business' IT systems, then exfiltrating their sensitive customer and process data.

5.3.3. Attractive fictitious profiles (AFPs) in times of war

Since 2010, there have been numerous cases where attractive fictitious profiles (AFPs) created on social networks were used to attract enemy users engaged in armed conflict, with the aim of collecting tactical or strategic information. These cyber-intelligence practices, initially without intruding into the enemy's systems, rely on social engineering techniques and attractive fictitious data structures that establish trust and then launch an involuntary transfer of information from the targets to the attacker. Confidence and "friendly" conversations then make it possible to send files (in .pdf or .doc format), install takeover software from a distance onto a computer or smartphone and exfiltrate data of a military nature.

An article from *Der Spiegel* appeared in May 2010 reporting an AFP operation attributed to Hezbollah targeting the Israeli Army. It would have made it possible, from a single fictitious profile created on Facebook, to extract the sensitive information of 200 soldiers or reservists at Tsahal.

In the same vein, in 2012, a study by the Australian defense department reported that a group of Taliban combatants had created an AFP and then used it to spy on Australian soldiers engaged within the international coalition.

The Syrian conflict and AFPs: in 2013–2014, the Syrian conflict saw the largest number of cyber-intelligence operations relying on AFPs. A study by the American cyber-intelligence firm FireEye highlighted a vast espionage campaign targeting rebel groups in the FSA (Free Syrian Army) opposing the regime of Bashar al-Assad. The report entitled "Behind the Syrian Conflict's Digital Front Lines", published on 2 February 2015 by FireEye showed how a group of unidentified attackers had collected a substantial volume of tactical and strategic data after using AFPs and injecting malicious codes into the targeted machines. Fake female profiles of "*femmes fatales*" were created on Skype and Facebook and adapted to the expectations of fighters' and commanders in the FSA rebellion. Researchers from FireEye discovered that more than 7.7 GB of data were captured during the operation. Documents in .pdf format containing malicious software for taking remote control of a computer were exchanged between the targets and the attacker. Data collection provided important elements of the Syrian opposition's strategy, battle plans, supply needs and a large volume of personal data on rebel combatants in the form of instant messaging sessions and .txt files containing reports of military operations underway. The operation that took place from November 2013 to January 2014 targeted both members of rebel groups linked to the FSA and groups of Islamists fighting on Syrian soil. More than 60 targets were identified, including the head of a combatant unit, a former high-ranking officer who had deserted Bashar al-Assad's security services, the local manager of a Turkish NGO, a member of a press center based in Syria and combatant personnel. During their conversations with the *"femmes fatales"* fictitious profiles, the attacker asked the target if he could use Skype on a computer or telephone. He was then sent an attractive photo accompanied by malware that was installed on opening the photo. The fictitious profiles were rigged with digital traps: malicious links camouflaged behind a discourse favorable to the Syrian opposition and highly relevant security instructions recommending the use of secure communication tools, VPNs (virtual private networks) and Tor as a network for anonymous communication.

Here, we find a good example of the art of war according to Sun Tzu 2.0 relying, according to FireEye, on a "digital Mata Hari". The attackers were able to display a ruse linking social engineering, AFPs and an effective "tailored" digital toolbox while still remaining technically simple and classic. The malware reused a known code circulating on the Internet, in particular, the "DarkComet" remote access Trojan, which has existed since 2008 and whose author is thought to be French. DarkComet was at that time an available and effective tool, not very discreet certainly, but still poorly detected or even undetected by the usual antivirus software. The attackers used a second malware, much more sophisticated than DarkComet, this time targeting the operating system for Android smartphones. They took advantage of the fact that frequent electricity cuts affecting installations on the ground pushed the rebels to store information on their smartphones rather than on a fixed machine, consuming much more energy and less easily rechargeable.

According to the team of researchers from FireEye, the group supervising the attack was probably located outside of Syrian territory. Several traces (algorithmic projections) were identified, suggesting that the attackers may have had links with Lebanon. A fake pro-rebellion, pro-Syrian opposition website, serving as a support for the AFPs and rigged with numerous malicious links was registered in Lebanon. Other traces pointing to Lebanon suggested that the attackers effectively acted from this country or that they chose Lebanon as a fictitious country of attribution. It is important to remember that it still remains very complex to attribute a cyber-attack with any certainty. There are only concordant indices, algorithmic projections that can be created from scratch to fool a future investigator. Algorithmically, the problem of attribution is equivalent, in complexity, to the problem, which has already been mentioned (see Chapter 4 section 1), of identifying an algorithmic projection.

Unlike the Syrian Electronic Army (SEA), a "hyper-hacktive" body from the start of the Syrian conflict in 2011 which almost always owned its own attacks, the group involved in this operation chose to remain as discreet and secretive as possible, in conformity with the nature of its mission. The information collected then gave the attacker an immediate tactical advantage on the battlefield. It should be noted that with this Syrian operation, the term "BD" (Battlespace Digitization) takes on its full meaning here!

5.3.4. An influence operation by AFPs against American soldiers, attributed to Russia

Revealed in June 2017, an influence operation using a set of female AFPs on Facebook was attributed (with all the precautions used regarding attribution) to a group of Russian cyber-activists. This operation specifically targeted the profiles of American soldiers engaged (or not) in the Iraqi and Syrian territory. Launching the operation classically relies on sending out invitations on Facebook to meet a female AFP, accompanied by a private message and a friend request to the targeted American soldier. The attacker's main aim lies in sending out pro-Russian propaganda messages inserted astutely and effectively into the newsfeed of targeted American soldiers. Thus, the story of a Russian soldier, killed heroically fighting against the Islamic State group, was spread widely on Facebook, via this fictitious profile structure. The influence worked perfectly, as the exemplary valor of the fighter sacrificing his life for his mission aroused great admiration among the ranks of American soldiers who read about it on their Facebook accounts. The aim was then achieved at the least operational cost.

In the United States, pro-Putin sentiment increased from 13% of favorable opinions in 2015 to 20% in 2017. Russian communication on social media certainly contributed to this but in a percentage, by its very nature, impossible to measure. Social networks remain an easy tool to access and insert oneself at little cost into a country's foreign and military policy.

During the Ukrainian crisis and the annexation of Crimea by Russia, Ukrainian soldiers were bombarded physically and digitally by means of a multitude of pro-Russian influence messages seeking to demotivate and demoralize them. The information war and the conflict's projection onto cyberspace accompanied the Ukrainian crisis from its start until just after it stabilized.

The Pentagon, according to one of its spokespersons, estimates that the risk of direct influence on American troops via social networks has increased considerably in the past 5 years. American soldiers are currently systematically sensitized and educated in the preventative detection of AFPs, to avoid them falling into the digital traps linked to them. China, Russia and Iran are often cited by US officials as regular users of influence AFPs but what about American or European operations, orchestrated by different groups of activists or state-sponsored officials? In his book "Cyber War" published in 2010, Richard Clarke, a former anti-terrorist advisor to the White House, reports that during the Iraq War in 2003, the American command inundated the inboxes of Iranian solders to invite them to put down arms and surrender. Clearly, these techniques were already an integral part of the set of digital influence tools formed of well-targeted malicious software and fictitious algorithmic projections.

5.3.5. *China, Sun Tzu and AFPs*

This affair is recent, dating from December 2017. The German intelligence services had just published a warning on the proliferation of AFPs supervised by groups of Chinese attackers who preferred to target high-level German personalities and politicians. The fictitious structure put in place was fairly sophisticated, combining AFPs, fake authentication platforms and fake information websites. The communiqué from the German security services emphasized the level of damage that an important target who falls into the trap would cause, involuntarily triggering an exfiltration of sensitive data to the attacker. A meticulous inquiry spanning approximately 9 months showed that more than 10,000 German citizens had been contacted on LinkedIn by AFPs of headhunters, recruiters, universities, influencers, think tanks and business directors. Among the fictitious profiles are those of "Rachel Li", a headhunter for "RiseHR", and "Alex Li", a project manager from the "Center for the development of Euro-Chinese studies". The most attractive profiles were able to establish relationships with high-level diplomats and politicians spread across the whole of Europe.

It is difficult, for want of hindsight, to evaluate precisely the number of citizens entrapped and whose personal data have been exfiltrated, but the number may be substantial given the large, initial base of the attack. This is also the reason why several Western intelligence agencies have expressed their fears about this type of operation, which could correlatively draw some agents to be recruited into the service of the attacking power on their own soil. The growth in the power of the artificial intelligence used to build highly immersive, coherent and global fictitious data structures will raise this risk and make it possible to industrialize future operations built on AFPs. The number of trapped targets could thus increase in scale, moving from several hundred to tens of thousands of victims. We do not doubt that artificial intelligence will also contribute to detecting these AFP operations very far ahead of time and that it will make it possible to halt them, in some cases.

6

High-impact Cyber-operations Built on Fictitious Algorithmic Projections

6.1. The Newscaster cyber-espionage operation – NewsOnLine

Cyber-espionage operations are becoming commonplace today and stick to extending a rationale of acquiring information that dates from the very first human conflict. Systemically, the complexity of digital space promotes the implementation of particularly intrusive and aggressive data collection. The Iranian operation Newscaster [BER 14] is emblematic for example: it unites digital secrecy, ruses and technology to fool and eavesdrop on targets and clearly proves the Persian proverb: "truth is separated from falsehood by a hair".

6.1.1. *A sophisticated operation*

In 2014, the American IT security and intelligence firm iSIGHT Partners highlighted and emphasized a large-scale cyber-intelligence operation targeting multiple American, Israeli, British and Saudi personalities. Newscaster began in 2011, relying on social networks in order to create fictitious profiles and build an information site as a hook, then attack its targets. The technical study carried out by iSIGHT Partners attributes the operation to a professional group of Iranian hackers. Deployed throughout, its level of complexity, its secrecy (it was active for three years) and the means used clearly suggest state expertise and supervision.

The increase of the operation's power was very progressive. As such, some see it as the Iranian response to the "Stuxnet" attack sustained by Teheran in 2010. Newscaster is first and foremost an operation in collecting closed data (cyber-espionage) directed against more high-ranking officers in the American army, decision-makers, journalists and American, Israeli, British and Saudi parliamentary representatives. More than 2,000 people have been connected to the false information network NewsOnAir since 2011 and have been trapped by viral loads transmitted by the site or during digital exchanges in which they were engaged (Keylogger, Trojan, crack, etc.). Once the target's accounts are hacked, secret programs for collecting and exporting data were installed and activated on their machines. A 4-star admiral in the Navy as well as embassy staff were victims of the attack.

6.1.2. Modus operandi

The attackers built a fictitious information network serving very gradually to instill confidence in the individuals targeted. The Newscaster strategy was long term, building a sophisticated and coherent architecture that inspired confidence. An information site "NewsOnAir" (newsonair.org) was specially developed which used fake journalists, fake contributors, published press articles and a fake network of subscribers to the site's newsletter. Fictitious users were created from scratch by attackers favoring profiles that would be compatible with the future victims' concerns and interests. Here, we can mention "super social engineering", adapted to the psychological profiles targeted. The search for global coherence in the assemblage guided its construction.

The "digitally probable", the fake credible and the production of admissible algorithmic projections (digital traces) were the keys to the success of the Newscaster operation. The fictitious profiles created by the attackers stated that they worked for the information site newsonair.org and suggested to the targets via their LinkedIn, Facebook, YouTube and Google accounts, that they join them and link them to the information network. The articles published on the NewSonAir site tended to demonstrate the seriousness of the fictitious American network. It often involved republishing press articles from the Associated Press, the BBC and Reuters. In addition to fake profiles of journalists, the attackers developed profiles of professionals in the defense sector. According to iSIGHT Partners, the newsonair.org site was registered in Teheran and hosted by an Iranian provider. Several hundred targets were directly impacted by the Newscaster operation. The group of 14 fictitious American profiles deployed on the main social networks (Figure 6.1) is presented in Table 6.1.

Figure 6.1. *Fake information site Newsonair*

These fictitious profiles made it possible to "phish" targets by making the Newscaster infrastructure truly dynamic. The overall coherence of the assemblage instilled confidence in future victims. The level of confidence engendered vulnerability and then enabled intrusion into and importation of private data.

Fictitious profile created by the attacker	Fictitious profession	Supports used on the social networks	Number of relationships on the support network
PF1 Sandra Maler	Reporter, NewsOnAir	LinkedIn, Facebook, Twitter, Google	226
PF2 Adia Mitchell	Reporter, NewsOnAir	LinkedIn, Facebook, Twitter, WordPress	281
PF3 Amanda Teysson	Reporter, NewsOnAir	LinkedIn, Facebook, Twitter, Google	310
PF4 Sara McKibben	Reporter, NewsOnAir	LinkedIn, Facebook	Unknown
PF5 Joseph Nilsson	Founder, NewsOnAir	LinkedIn, Facebook	231
PF6 Jane Baker (Ava T. Foster)	Reporter, NewsOnAir	LinkedIn	30
PF7 Mary Cole	Recruiter for a defense contractor	LinkedIn, Facebook, Google	>500
PF8 Berna Achando	Web Designer for a defense contractor	LinkedIn, Facebook	151
PF9 Jeann Maclkin	Systems administrator for the US Navy	LinkedIn, Facebook, Blogger, YouTube	>500
PF10 Alfred Nilsson	Talent acquisition for a defense contractor	LinkedIn, Facebook	Unknown
PF11 Josh Nilsson (Josh Furie)	IT manager for a defense contractor	LinkedIn, Facebook	130
PF12 Dorotha Baasch	IT analyst for a defense contractor	LinkedIn, Facebook	Unknown
PF13 Kenneth Babcock	Fiscal advisor for a payment body	LinkedIn, Facebook, Google	Unknown
PF14 Donnie Eadense	Manager of a defense contractor's IT system	LinkedIn	118

Table 6.1. *Group of 14 fictitious American profiles deployed on the main social networks*

6.1.3. *Confidence that arises from time and coherence*

Newscaster began in 2011 by creating the information site Newsonair and publishing the core of its fictitious profiles. Cyber-entrapment then came into play and the first targets began to be impacted, without being aware of it. To survive, such a construction should constantly demonstrate a high overall coherence. A single contradiction detected in the core profiles or on the fictitious site may be enough to alert and end the operation.

Newscaster's authors were necessarily confronted with the coherence test at any scale or dimension:

– spatial coherence, which involves data and links published on the infrastructure's various supports and

– temporal coherence, which aims to maintain good chronologies in describing events, in constructing messages and communicating with targets.

The profiles were created according to standard models of the algorithmic projections of individuals who were compatible with the future targets. The profile of the American journalist, connected and active on social networks, is part of it and also that of the expert in the defense domain. In fact, it reassures the reader by projecting rigor, seriousness and security onto future exchanges.

These profiles were constructed carefully depending on the targeted profiles. Links based on similarities (shared areas of interest, shared professional domains, shared culture) are established by the Newscaster architects to create adhesion and attractiveness in victims. There too, care should be taken to maintain overall coherence and to chase up micro-contradictions that could come to sabotage the operation. The Newsonair information site then comes into play as a unifying space within the device. It brings confirmation, expertise and cohesion to the whole and acts as a catalyst for confidence.

If a systemic approach is used to analyze an operation such as Newscaster, we quickly detect the paradox that increases the duration of the setup's validity: the more the fictitious network develops in the size and volume of connection with targets, the more the confidence instilled is "visible" from the outside. However, the more the fictitious body is broadened, the more it provides space on which contradictions and incoherences may appear. This subtle paradox should be linked to the concepts of complexity and anti-fragility that are at the forefront of any cyber-manipulation operation.

6.2. Attacks by HoaxCrash and false transfer orders: the power of the cognitive lure

6.2.1. *The human factor and cognitive lure: the keys to HoaxCrash and false transfer order attacks*

The human factor is often evoked to indicate the weak link in a data system's security chain. The exploitation of human vulnerabilities installs and maintains the threat. Cognitive biases, credulity, sometimes naivety and all of the minor lapses that each of us is guilty of at one time or another in their digital activity, are examples of biological vulnerabilities that the attacker knows how to exploit.

When we speak of social engineering, it is implied that this attacker puts into place a strategy, the aim of which is to obtain information about the system that they wish to target. The human factor is often therefore the first mechanism to be activated to obtain key data for a future intrusion. On the contrary, sometimes, the attacker does not await any data feedback to carry out their operation, but limits themselves to circulating a more or less sophisticated set of credible and coherent false data. Their belief that this is a valid body of information then engenders a series of actions desired by the attacker, who will be able to exploit them.

This cognitive lure mechanism can trigger strong turbulence in an environment that is hyper-connected and saturated with information. This is found in false transfer order attacks, BEC (business email compromise scams) attacks, attacks changing bank details and attacks by HoaxCrash, whose immediate and scalable impact may be global.

The acceleration of the diffusion of information today involves all sectors of human activity, in particular the economy and finance. By relying on fluidity and reactivity in exchanges, this acceleration, by nature systemic, has opened up new spaces for interaction in "high-frequency" mode and, correlatively, created new vulnerabilities.

Although influence and misinformation operations have always formed part of the history of communication since Antiquity, they are now prospering on digital infrastructures and are fed by the deluge of data. Hoaxes, practiced by the Greeks and Romans, have traveled across two millennia to become a powerful tool for influence and manipulation.

When it is used to destabilize the price of a share by creating artificial volatility on stock, it is therefore called a "HoaxCrash" (Hoax for the Hoax and Crash for the resulting stock market flash crash). Such cyber-operations merit particular attention as the turbulence that they cause is often very violent and costly for the victims of the attack.

Starting with the HoaxCrash that targeted the Vinci group on 22 November 2016, it is instructive to review earlier cases and then to analyze this type of cyber-attack. This analysis shows in particular that a HoaxCrash can be defined formally by data from three parameters: the duration of its validity, its effectiveness and its power.

False data are also being used more and more often to fool human operators and lead them to make transfers to fraudulent accounts. False transfer order-type attacks, BEC attacks and attacks changing back details have multiplied since 2010, impacting numerous businesses.

The overall damage in France has exceeded 485 million euros with hundreds of SMEs and SMIs ensnared and more than 2300 complaints lodged over the last 5 years. Automatic detection of fictitious data structures is therefore a major challenge in cybersecurity.

6.2.2. Attacks using HoaxCrash

6.2.2.1. The case of the Vinci HoaxCrash

On Tuesday, November 22 at around 4pm, the Vinci group was the target of an operation aiming to destabilize the prices of its shares via publication of an "official" fake press release transmitted to stock market operators. This fake message (Figure 6.2) sent by the specialist press agency Bloomberg reported a warning of a review of accounts consolidated in 2015 and the first half of 2016 as well as the removal of Vinci's financial director, after the discovery of accounting errors affecting more than 3.5 billion euros. Vinci's stock then dropped almost instantly by 18.28% (Figures 6.3 and 6.4), from 61.81 euros to 49.93 euros in a few minutes. The group's value went from around 36 billion euros on Tuesday, November 22 in the morning to 29 billion euros at the height of its undoing, which represents a momentary loss of more than seven billion euros.

The first denial by Vinci came (by telephone) at 4.10pm, which is only five minutes after the initial publication of the Hoax by Bloomberg. The second official denial was published by Vinci at 4.49pm on its Internet site:

"A fake Vinci press release was published by Bloomberg on 22nd November at 4.05pm. Vinci formally denies all the 'information' in this fake release and is considering forms of legal action to pursue following this publication".

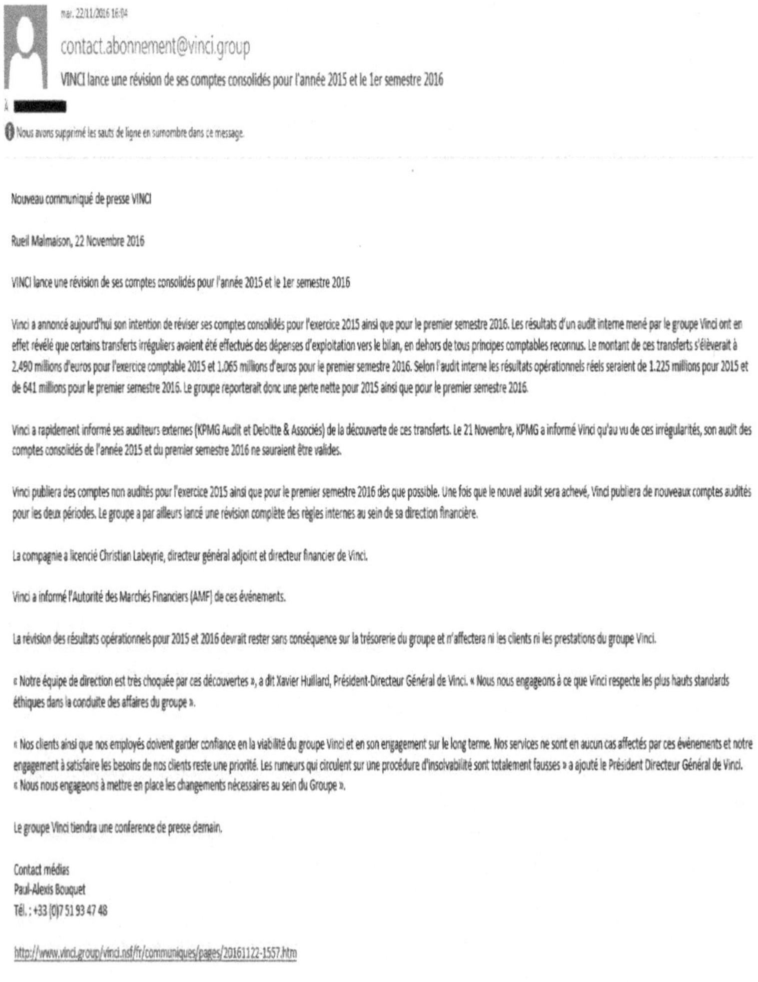

mar. 22/11/2016 16:04

contact.abonnement@vinci.group

VINCI lance une révision de ses comptes consolidés pour l'année 2015 et le 1er semestre 2016

À ▓▓▓▓▓▓

ⓘ Nous avons supprimé les sauts de ligne en surnombre dans ce message.

Nouveau communiqué de presse VINCI

Rueil Malmaison, 22 Novembre 2016

VINCI lance une révision de ses comptes consolidés pour l'année 2015 et le 1er semestre 2016

Vinci a annoncé aujourd'hui son intention de réviser ses comptes consolidés pour l'exercice 2015 ainsi que pour le premier semestre 2016. Les résultats d'un audit interne mené par le groupe Vinci ont en effet révélé que certains transferts irréguliers avaient été effectués des dépenses d'exploitation vers le bilan, en dehors de tous principes comptables reconnus. Le montant de ces transferts s'élèverait à 2,490 millions d'euros pour l'exercice comptable 2015 et 1,065 millions d'euros pour le premier semestre 2016. Selon l'audit interne les résultats opérationnels réels seraient de 1,225 millions pour 2015 et de 641 millions pour le premier semestre 2016. Le groupe reporterait donc une perte nette pour 2015 ainsi que pour le premier semestre 2016.

Vinci a rapidement informé ses auditeurs externes (KPMG Audit et Deloitte & Associés) de la découverte de ces transferts. Le 21 Novembre, KPMG a informé Vinci qu'au vu de ces irrégularités, son audit des comptes consolidés de l'année 2015 et du premier semestre 2016 ne sauraient être valides.

Vinci publiera des comptes non audités pour l'exercice 2015 ainsi que pour le premier semestre 2016 dès que possible. Une fois que le nouvel audit sera achevé, Vinci publiera de nouveaux comptes audités pour les deux périodes. Le groupe a par ailleurs lancé une révision complète des règles internes au sein de sa direction financière.

La compagnie a licencié Christian Labeyrie, directeur général adjoint et directeur financier de Vinci.

Vinci a informé l'Autorité des Marchés Financiers (AMF) de ces événements.

La révision des résultats opérationnels pour 2015 et 2016 devrait rester sans conséquence sur la trésorerie du groupe et n'affectera ni les clients ni les prestations du groupe Vinci.

« Notre équipe de direction est très choquée par ces découvertes », a dit Xavier Huillard, Président-Directeur Général de Vinci. « Nous nous engageons à ce que Vinci respecte les plus hauts standards éthiques dans la conduite des affaires du groupe ».

« Nos clients ainsi que nos employés doivent garder confiance en la viabilité du groupe Vinci et en son engagement sur le long terme. Nos services ne sont en aucun cas affectés par ces événements et notre engagement à satisfaire les besoins de nos clients reste une priorité. Les rumeurs qui circulent sur une procédure d'insolvabilité sont totalement fausses » a ajouté le Président Directeur Général de Vinci. « Nous nous engageons à mettre en place les changements nécessaires au sein du Groupe ».

Le groupe Vinci tiendra une conférence de presse demain.

Contact médias
Paul-Alexis Bouquet
Tél. : +33 (0)7 51 93 47 48

http://www.vinci.group/vinci.nsf/fr/communiques/pages/20161122-1557.htm

Figure 6.2. *Fake message used after the Vinci HoaxCrash and link to the fictitious site www.vinci.group. For an English translation of this figure, see the Appendix*

Figure 6.3. *Changes in Vinci stock from July 15 to November 22 2016.*
For a color version of this figure, see www.iste.co.uk/berthier/digital.zip

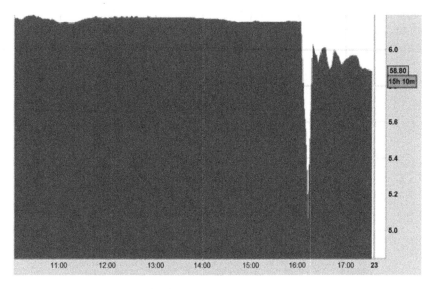

Figure 6.4. *Profile of the Vinci flash crash from November 22 2016.*
For a color version of this figure, see www.iste.co.uk/berthier/digital.zip

The attacker published their own "fake denial" at 4.27pm with the aim of creating and exploiting peak volatility on the shares. Vinci's stock ended trading on the Tuesday evening at 58.80 euros, a decline of 3.76%, for a total volume of exchanges reaching five times those carried out on average in a "normal" context. Vinci lodged a complaint against X on the same day as the attack and informed the Financial Markets Authority (FMA). This should precisely identify the identity of the operators (human or HFT robots) who have exploited this destabilization, i.e. those who were present and active at the right moment, in the right place, during the operation.

Finally, it will be noted that a message denying the operation destabilization Vinci's shares was sent during the attack on 22/11 and sent to the press on November 23: "*Market-media action against Vinci: claim – the forest at* Notre-Dame-des-Landes *has itself experienced concrete falling and its occupants celebrated this new blow brought directly against this concrete monster's shares*". It makes sense to consider this message with full precaution before use, taking account especially of the operational capacities of the Zadists, opponents to the future airport of Notre-Dame-des-Landes. It is highly possible and probable that this claim also comes from the opportunist scam.

The operation seems to have been constructed to create great volatility in an artificial way on Vinci's stock and then to exploit these variations to profit from them. The chronology of the HoaxCrash shows that the useful period for the attack is no more than 8 min after publication of the fake message.

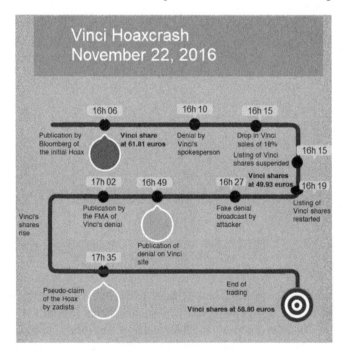

Figure 6.5. *Chronology of the attack on Vinci by HoaxCrash*

It will be noted that the flash crash triggered on Vinci's stock did not have repercussions on other stock market values. This absence of contagion for the market is essentially due to the very targeted nature of the Hoax and the rapid denial published by the attacker and then by Vinci. The Hoax publication sequence, some minutes after the denial, demonstrates that the attacker only sought volatility on the targeted stock and the flash crash with the sole objective of short-term speculative profit. This "Hoax–denial" sequence also rules out the objective of a simple crash (without a rise) of Vinci's shares, which would have been the objective of a group of activists with ecological or political motivations.

The Vinci group's communication office reacted very quickly, from the fourth minute of the attack, by producing denials by telephone to press agencies and then by publishing an official release on its site, 40 minutes later. Looking at this crisis management chronology, it seems difficult to reduce any further the human reaction time faced with a HoaxCrash attempt. Only an algorithmic response, at high frequency and with a broad spectrum of dissemination, would make it possible to stop the process in its own timescale, before it has had any effect on the markets.

The Vinci HoaxCrash should make us query more generally the responsibility of the media, the specialist press, financial information portals and social networks in the validation and diffusion of information. The sensitivity and reactivity of audiences faced with digital data, verified or otherwise, seem intimately linked to the system's vulnerability when it is confronted with disinformation and influence operations that are sometimes very rudimentary in their design. How do we define a chain of responsibility that takes account both of "high-frequency" timescales and the impact of fake information on hyper-sensitive, interconnected systems? It is finally the question of resilience or anti-fragility [TAL 12] defined by Nassim Nicholas Taleb that should be asked about HoaxCrash mechanisms.

6.2.2.2. HoaxCrash mechanisms

A HoaxCrash always begins with the publication of a "Hoax" using the theft of an authority figure's identity. This false information, believed to be legitimate by stock market operators, then triggers a flash crash of the targeted business's shares. The HoaxCrash's operational mode is carried out according to the following sequence: the attacker begins by stealing the identity of a member of the management of an industrial group X trading on the exchange. They write a "credible" warning message imitating as well as possible the business' communication channel. This warning, signed in the name of one of its leaders, reveals financial difficulties or embezzlement in the group's activities. It is immediately disseminated to specialist press agencies such as Bloomberg and the main stock market operators. If the message does not trigger any doubts, the effect is immediate: X's share price plummets suddenly. Some minutes later, a second release emitted by the attacker refutes the first warning, which triggers the immediate rise of the stock price. This volatility, controlled over time, is then exploited by a second actor, the accomplice of the attacker or sponsor of the HoaxCrash, who profits from the artificial variations caused by the market believing the fake warning. The data and time advantage, created from scratch by the attacker, enables them to make very considerable profits from the fluctuations in the stock, of which they had prior knowledge. Finally, high-frequency trading (HFT) is often mentioned as the operation's third actor since it is capable of amplifying and benefitting from the flash crash born of the false information.

This type of operation to destabilize a stock exchange did not start with the Vinci affair.

In April 2013, the Syrian Electronic Army (SEA) took control of the official Twitter account of the Associated Press agency. A fake message was then published on the pirated account that an explosion had taken place at the White House and that Barack Obama was injured. The fake tweet triggered an immediate drop in all Western exchanges in the form of a flash crash at Wall Street to the tune of 136 billion dollars and a drop in Standard & Poor's 500 share index by 145 points in 3 min [BER 15c].

Some analysts rapidly attributed the violence of this flash crash to high-frequency trading, but an in-depth inquiry has shown that orders were passed above all by human operators who were gripped by panic [BER 14].

Figure 6.7 represents the drop (in the shape of a V) in the Dow Jones index some instants after publication of the SEA's Hoax.

Figure 6.6. *SEA's fake tweet in the name of the Associated Press agency*

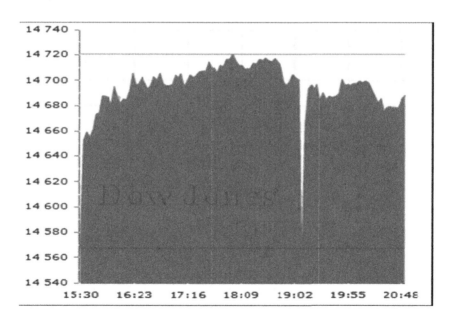

Figure 6.7. *Flash crash of the Dow Jones triggered by the SEA's fake tweet.
For a color version of this figure, see www.iste.co.uk/berthier/digital.zip*

In 2013, it was the Australian group Whitehaven Coal who sustained an attack from a group of militant ecologists. The latter stole the identity of one of the group's managers and sent a fake press release announcing that one of Whitehaven Coal's mining sites was not profitable. The stock's share price then collapsed temporarily.

In 2014, the security firm G4S, responsible for security at refugee and migrant camps, sustained the same type of attack. A fake press release created via identity theft announced that the firm had encountered difficulties that it was going to revise its accounts from 2013 and that its financial director had been removed from his post. The price of G4S's shares dropped after publication of this fake warning.

In 2015, the American group Avon (Figure 6.8) was in turn targeted by the publication of a fake message announcing a takeover bid (OPA) that destabilized the price of its stock and forced Avon to deny the OPA urgently.

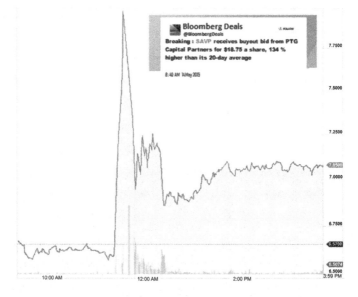

Figure 6.8. *Disruption of Avon's shares in 2015. For a color version of this figure, see www.iste.co.uk/berthier/digital.zip*

In November 2016, the American firm Fitbit saw the price of its shares strongly disrupted by the publication of a fake release announcing an offer to buy up the company by the Chinese investment fund ABM Capital.

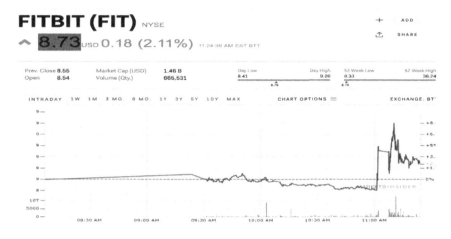

Figure 6.9. *Disruption of the Fitbit share price following a fake press release. For a color version of this figure, see www.iste.co.uk/berthier/digital.zip*

The motivations of the authors of the HoaxCrash were varied, as shown in the following table.

HoaxCrash	Motivation(s) of the attacker
SEA-AP (2013)	Politics – Hacktivism (Syrian conflict)
Whitehaven Coal (2013)	Politics – activism by a group of ecologists
G4S (2014)	Politics – activism
Avon (2015)	Economics – (damage to image – speculation)
Fitbit (2016)	Economics and activism
Vinci (2016)	Economics (volatility – speculation)

The price of the crypto-currency Bitcoin was targeted during several attacks using HoaxCrash. The last dated from September 11, 2017. False information stating that the Chinese authorities were preparing to ban platforms from exchanging Bitcoin on their territory was relayed by the American press. The fake news triggered an immediate drop in the value of the crypto-currency and then a rise after its denial.

6.2.2.3. Efficiency and power of a HoaxCrash

It is possible to define the effectiveness and power of a HoaxCrash built on the publication of a message "m" containing false information relating to the activity of an industrial group trading on the stock exchange.

6.2.2.3.1. Effectiveness of a HoaxCrash

The effectiveness of a HoaxCrash is obtained by dividing the net gain $G(m)$ obtained by the attacker by the algorithmic complexity of the message m and the body of information $S(m)$ that it broadcasts to carry out its attack.

$$E(m) = G(m, S(m))/K(m, S(m))$$

where $G(m, S(m))$ designates the (net) gain obtained by the attacker after carrying out the following sequence:

1) Possible creation of a publication support $S(m)$ imitating the target's official communication support or taking control of (hacking) a legitimate communication support.

2) Publication of the message m (the Hoax) on the support $S(m)$.

3) Exploiting variations in the price of the targeted shares and order passing for the duration of the HoaxCrash's effectiveness.

4) Attainment of gain $G(m, S(m))$ by the attacker.

$K(m, S(m))$ designates the algorithmic complexity (Kolmogorov complexity) of the published message and its publication support created specifically for the operation.

6.2.2.3.2. Impact of a HoaxCrash on a share

A HoaxCrash's impact is obtained by dividing the total value of variations in the targeted share price A (evaluated once the flash crash has ended after publication of the official denial) by the complexity already cited.

$$P(m) = V(A, T(m))/K(m, S(m))$$

where A designates the targeted share, $T(m)$ is the Hoax's duration of validity before publication of the official denial and $V(A, T(m))$ is the total value of variations in the price of the share A evaluated after publication of the official denial, once the flash crash has ended.

A HoaxCrash $H(m)$ is therefore quantitatively and qualitatively determined by data from the triplet $H(m) = \{ T(m), P(m), E(m) \}$.

The morphology of HoaxCrash-type attacks risks evolving by complexifying significantly. Imitation techniques already make it possible to reproduce some websites identically by retaining an apparent address similar to the official, targeted address. This is the data infrastructure used upstream to make the fake message credible, which will require the most substantial effort on the part of the attacker.

High-impact platforms for validating information and detecting HoaxCrashes will be capable, thanks to artificial intelligence, of detecting the most rudimentary fake messages in real time. They will therefore produce a warning that will avert the flash crash.

6.2.3. False transfer order and BEC attacks

6.2.3.1. False transfer order, BEC, lucrative and targeted attacks

A "BEC" attack consists, for scammers, of convincing the employee of a business to urgently carry out a substantial transfer to a third party in order to obey a pretend order from their boss, under the pretext of paying a debt, honoring a contract or some other reason.

For the fraudsters, *"changing bank account details"* consists of sending an email to an employee in the accounting department or treasury, posing as a provider, and asking them to direct their payments to another bank account, belonging to the scammers.

Carried out by telephone or by email, the false bank transfer order scam affects businesses of any size and any sector. Often located abroad, the scammer collects the maximum amount of intelligence on the business in advance. This knowledge of the business, combined with a persuasive and convincing tone, is the key to the scam's success. The operation is then launched, targeting individuals who are capable of operating transfers (accounting services, treasury, secretaries, etc.).

First appearing in France since 2010, false transfer order or BEC attacks were some of the targeted attacks requiring a good knowledge of the targeted business, its personnel and its directorship.

The initial social engineering phase was thus paramount for the digital scam to run properly. It makes it possible to collect information on the business' commercial activity, its production, providers, customers and organigram. Once this data collection has been carried out, the attacker sends electronic messages and requests by telephone, demanding the urgent transfer of a substantial sum of money to an international account. Generally, they complain about the delay or non-payment of an invoice or service payment stealing the identity of an authority or trusted third party. The message is almost always "confidential and urgent". The main targets of these messages are assistants or executive assistants, accounting secretaries and personnel in the accounting departments of SMEs and SMIs.

Substantial work creating sensitization to false transfer order attempts has proven necessary for the personnel exposed to them. That said, this sensitization may not be enough to reduce risk and should necessarily be paired with automatic detection solutions.

6.2.3.2. Statistics involving BEC

Since 2010, BEC (business email compromise) or "changing bank account details" scams have had many victims among French businesses. Several hundred false transfer order or attempted false transfer order attacks have been listed, with overall damage of 485 million euros.

The French Central Office for Combating Large-scale Financial Crime (*Office Central de Répression de la Grande Délinquance Financière*, OCRGDF) calls businesses to greater vigilance:

> "*It is a real economic scourge. One must be vigilant, the Christmas period is often synonymous with laxity in businesses and scammers benefit from it.*"[1]

Over the last five years, 2,300 complaints have been lodged. That said, many businesses do not dare to lodge a complaint for fear of negative publicity and of tainting their image. They have chosen to accept the damage without producing a legal response to the fraud.

The National Association of Financial Directors and Management (*Association Nationale des Directeurs Financiers et de Contrôle de Gestion*,

---

1 https://www.police-nationale.interieur.gouv.fr/Actualites/Dossiers/Cybercrime/L-arnaque-au-president-ou-escroquerie-aux-faux-ordres-de-virement-FOVI.

DFCG) has produced a barometer for business fraud in collaboration with Euler Hermes, the credit-assurance director [HAG 17].

Published at the end of 2016, this inquest revealed that 93% of French businesses had been victims of at least one attempted fraud in 2015 and that one in two had faced a BEC attack. These attacks took place most often during holiday periods when staff numbers were reduced and when vigilance was relaxed. Their increase in frequency was marked, since in 2014 only 77% of businesses were targeted.

More worrying in terms of the damage, is that on one occasion in three, the attempted attack was not foiled, the victim was not able to detect the fraud and the transfer was made. The common denominator of these attacks remains the initial identity theft that aims to instill confidence in an employee of the targeted business. Every type of authority can be evoked by the attacker in the fraudulent message to create a climate of trust and urgency: there could be a fake lawyer, banker, provider, accounts auditor and business director within a BEC attack.

The attacker must convince their target, by telephone or email, to carry out a transfer to a given account or modify the bank details of the recipient of the payment (attack by changing bank details). Their capacity for persuasion is thus critical for the operation to unfold successfully. For this reason, they always carry out preliminary research on the business, its activity and its customers. They then target personnel who are able to carry out payments and bank transactions (an employee of a financial service, an accounting agent, an assistant or executive assistant for a small business).

The DFCG has produced a list of common sense recommendations that make it possible to limit risk. Some of them can be automated:

– Sensitizing and encouraging employees not to communicate information relating to the running of the business and its customers on social networks.

– Sensitizing personnel in telephone contact with those outside (switchboard, buying managers, accounts).

– Putting in place systematic verifications and multiple signatures for international payments.

– Implementing confirmation requests before any unplanned operation that involves sending funds.

– In case of a request made by email, sending an email to the usual address of whoever has made the order, rather than simply replying to the initial request.

– Enhancing vigilance during holiday and vacation periods and when staff numbers are reduced.

Finally, when the targeted employee makes the transfer without having detected the BEC attack, it is then necessary to warn the bank as quickly as possible and lodge a complaint with the police.

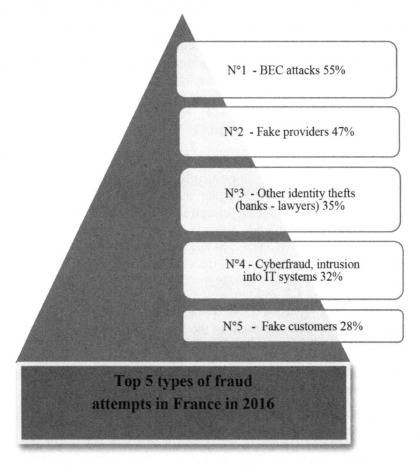

Figure 6.10. *Ranking of the top five fraud attempt types in France in 2016*

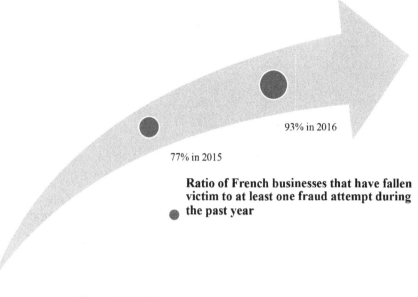

Figure 6.11. *Evolution of the ratio of businesses affected by fraud attempts in 2015–2016*

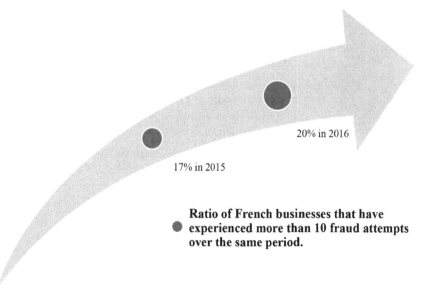

Figure 6.12. *Evolution of the ratio of businesses affected by more than 10 fraud attempts in 2015–2016*

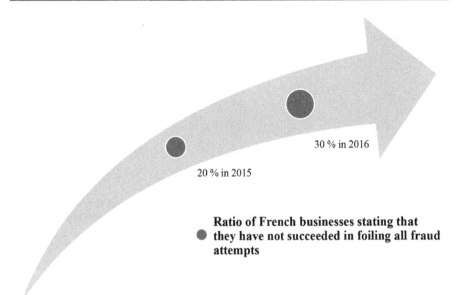

30 % in 2016

20 % in 2015

Ratio of French businesses stating that
they have not succeeded in foiling all fraud
attempts

Figure 6.13. *Evolution of the ratio of businesses affected by fraud in 2015–2016*

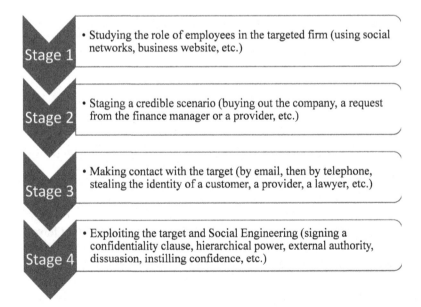

Stage 1
- Studying the role of employees in the targeted firm (using social networks, business website, etc.)

Stage 2
- Staging a credible scenario (buying out the company, a request from the finance manager or a provider, etc.)

Stage 3
- Making contact with the target (by email, then by telephone, stealing the identity of a customer, a provider, a lawyer, etc.)

Stage 4
- Exploiting the target and Social Engineering (signing a confidentiality clause, hierarchical power, external authority, dissuasion, instilling confidence, etc.)

Figure 6.14. *Chronological breakdown of the false
transfer order type built from fictitious algorithmic projections*

At a global level, the SYMANTEC study on BEC Scammers published in 2016 emphasizes a great increase in attacks built on false data and identity theft. BEC and false transfer order scams mainly affect small and medium-sized businesses (38%), regardless of their sectors of activity. On a daily basis, worldwide, more than 400 businesses have been the victims of attempted scams of the false transfer order type, with at least two employees in the firm targeted by fraudulent emails.

According to statistics from the FBI in 2016, the total damage would exceed three billion dollars, affecting more than 22,000 firms that were victims of false transfer order scams. At the root of these false transfer order scams are developments of the famous Nigerian fraud (code 419), already used on all continents.

Country of origin of false transfer order fraud – SCAM 419	Global distribution (sources: Symantec – FBI)
Nigeria	46%
The United States	27%
The United Kingdom	15%
South Africa	9%
Malaysia	2%
Russia	1%

The (English) words that appear most often in messages used by the authors of false transfer order scams are: "Request" (25%), "Payment" (15%), "Urgent" (10%), "Transfer Request" (9%), "URGENT" (8%), "Transfer Inquiry" (8%), "Payment Request" (6%), "Transfer Payment" (6%), "Urgent Request" (6%) and "REQUEST" (6%). The frequency with which these words characterizing false transfer order scams appear can contribute to their automatic detection via a semantic analysis platform that "reads" the messages.

6.2.4. Automatic detection of attacks by HoaxCrash and false transfer orders

6.2.4.1. Possible approaches in the fight against HoaxCrashes and false transfer order scams

The fight against the spread of false information on social networks is overtaking the priorities of cybersecurity for large digital actors. Thus,

Google and Facebook have just announced the development of specific tools for detecting the fake and authenticating the real. Facebook also wishes to forbid advertizing on pages which peddles false information. Google will dereference sites containing Hoaxes intended to fool and direct the public. Consideration of false data seems to have become widespread, notably after the election of Donald Trump. That said, prior detection of false information remains technically complex.

Fighting against the HoaxCrash consists of implementing measures for detecting false messages on a "high-frequency" timescale. Even when the denial is broadcast only 10 min after the initial publication of the Hoax, the "harm is done", since these 10 min are broadly enough to disrupt and influence the stock markets. It is therefore necessary to align the frequency of combating the HoaxCrash with that of the operation itself, by developing software agents that are active in real time, capable of measuring the instantaneous veracity of a message and evaluating its potential impact on the market if it is fraudulent.

Like spam detectors, the agent evaluates the veracity of a message by attributing to it an instantaneous probability of veracity depending on its form, its content and the external context. This measurement of veracity can then be built according to the following two approaches.

The first approach is based on putting in place a network of "corresponding agents" covering all actors on the stock market and listed companies. The agent evaluating a message should be able to ask a "corresponding" agent within the business or the administration named in the message, in order to obtain validation or repudiation of the message. Setting up such a network of agents communicating specifically on the veracity of messages that will impact the market will make it possible to optimize system reaction times and produce the automated publication of a denial in the case of HoaxCrash. The construction of a network of "corresponding" agents could also rely on a blockchain-type architecture to avoid the need for centralized supervision, which is often expensive and potentially vulnerable.

The second approach comes into play independently or in the absence of any confirmation or refutation of the "legitimate" corresponding agent. The evaluating agent is content enough with the message, its content, its metadata and the external context to assign to it a veracity value that, below a certain threshold, triggers warning and refutation of the message over the whole network.

In the context of the Vinci HoaxCrash, the initial message showed particularities that would have been easily detected by a software agent: the telephone number of the Vinci press officer at the end of the message was erroneous and the address of the site publishing the message appeared as "vinci.group", whereas the legitimate address of the Vinci group is "vinci.com".

Sometimes, there are errors in the text's spelling or grammatical style that should serve as a warning. In the case of the Vinci HoaxCrash, these elements were enough to cast doubt over the veracity of the message, but the haste that prevails within specialist financial press agencies (such as Bloomberg) and the human factor overrode the principle of precaution.

This observation makes it necessary to evaluate messages using a network of software agents. The use of solutions based on automated learning [BIR 09] can also strengthen the detection of fake communications by referring this time to historical, legitimate releases from the groups concerned. By cross-referencing and combining several algorithmic methods, it becomes possible to evaluate the veracity of the message precisely.

Scams that use the spreading of cognitive lures are growing in power. They cost economies dearly by causing damage that can put the survival of an SME in danger.

In the near future, it will be necessary to await the complexification of fictitious data structures on which the attacker will rely to carry out their operation. Automatic detection of fakes, at high frequency, will be the only pertinent response, accompanied by sensitization of personnel to biases and cognitive lures.

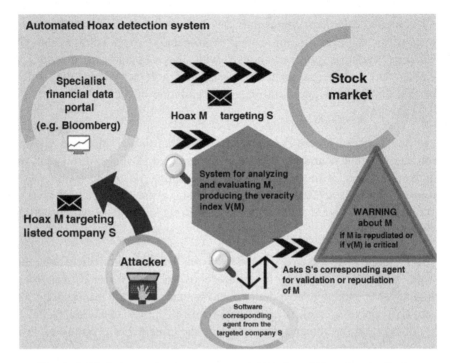

Figure 6.15. *Schema showing automated detection of HoaxCrash attacks. For a color version of this figure, see www.iste.co.uk/berthier/digital.zip*

Perspectives: fictitious data structures used as cognitive lures in the course of a cyber-attack should be subject to generalized detection. To do this, it is necessary to extend fake data detectors to the domains of images and videos.

The automatic detection of false and manipulated data is becoming a priority for non-state security. The risks of destabilization are substantial, as shown by the recent demonstration of a deep-learning platform producing an almost perfect video of a fictitious speech by Barack Obama. At the end of 2016, a research program was launched by the American agency DARPA to develop platforms for automatically detecting manipulated images and fake videos (MediFor program, Media Forensic).

Prospective Epilogue: Global Algorithmic Projection and NBIC Convergence

In the near future, how will our global algorithmic projections evolve under the joint effects of progress in artificial intelligence (AI) and the convergence of NBIC technologies (nanotechnology, biotechnology, IT and cognitive science)?

This question about the future should be explored from the angle of the different technological convergences that are rapidly transforming our environment and bringing together two spaces, the digital and the physical, which are overlapping and will end by fusing into a single ubiquitous space. A product of NBIC convergence, this space formed of atoms and forming the matter that carries information verifies the entropy principle.

7.1. A word on entropy

As a mathematical object, Shannon entropy is applied to the quantity of information contained or delivered by a data source (a computer file sent, an electrical signal, a text formulated in a language according to a fixed alphabet). It corresponds to the uncertainty that accompanies this message transmission.

For the receiver of the information, the more the source of transmission transmits different, non-redundant information, the more the entropy (or uncertainty on what the source transmits) increases. On the other hand, the more redundant the message, the more the associated entropy decreases. A minimal entropy corresponds to the context in which a source proceeds to a constant transmission by always sending the same symbol to the receiver, which knows what it ought to receive. There is no longer uncertainty regarding the message received. The more the receiver receives redundant information on a transmitted message, the more the entropy associated with the transmission of this message decreases. In contrast, when, for a source, all the symbols used are equi-probable, the entropy is maximal.

In physics, and more specifically in thermodynamics, entropy corresponds to a size associated with a system (an extensive state function) that characterizes the degree of disorganization or unpredictability in this physical system's data content.

The entropy principle predicts an inevitable evolution toward disorder and then a rise in entropy.

Any prospective thinking on the evolution of global algorithmic projection in the long term should consider the entropy principle, which applies to the ubiquitous space born of NBIC convergence.

7.2. Technology convergences and the spread of artificial intelligence to domains of human expertise

The convergence of technical and scientific disciplines is creating a dynamic that favors progress and innovation. The increase in the power of nanotechnology, biotechnology, IT and cognitive science relies on the interdisciplinary collaborations that contribute to bringing together and enriching the underlying technologies.

This marked trend has given rise to the concepts of NBIC and then CKTS, which can also be observed under the aegis of the spread of artificial intelligence to domains of human expertise.

7.3. NBIC convergence

The concept of the convergence of NBIC technological domains (nanotechnology, biotechnology, IT, cognitive science) was first mentioned in 2002 in a report of nearly 500 pages edited by the American National Science Foundation (NSF) [ROC 03]. This detailed and reasoned study acknowledged the necessary reconciliation of scientific knowledge in NBIC domains. It set the tone for the various civilian and military R&D programs that would follow over the next 15 years.

The dynamic of NBIC convergence can be summarized by a schema (Figure 7.1) that shows the following two partitions:

– the first partition separates the domain of physics on the left and that of biology on the right;

– the second partition separates elements related to hardware (above) from elements more like software (below).

While nanotechnology manipulates atoms, biotechnology is applied to genes, IT relies on bits and the cognitive science relies on biological neurons.

NBIC convergence designates the integration and superposition of these four domains in terms of technological innovation. A discovery in one of the four domains causes advances in the other three by bringing problems together and sharing approaches. IT and artificial intelligence act as binding agents and catalysts for this convergence.

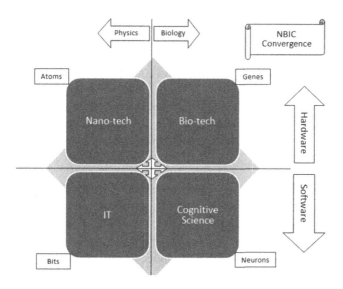

Figure 7.1. *NBIC convergence*

At the intersection of IT and biotechnology, nano-bio-informatics, calculations on DNA, sequencing and proteomics are developing. The intersection of biotechnology and nanotechnology materializes in nano-bio-medicine [CUR 16], nano-bio-technologies, synthetic biology and bio-photonics [EST 16]. Cognitive science and nanotechnology interact in neuromorphic engineering, intelligent environments and objects dedicated to cognitive development. Finally, information science and computer science collaborate with cognitive science in large-scale brain simulation programs, modeling cyber-conflict and personalized education.

The study of NBIC convergence relies on the definition of adapted metrics, making it possible to evaluate its speed and the distances separating the domains involved.

7.4. CKTS

It was in 2009 that the concept of CKTS appeared, which generalized and extended the perimeter of NBIC convergence [ROC 13]. CKTS (convergence of knowledge and technology to benefit society) introduces a societal dimension by postulating the benefits of knowledge and technology for the benefit of humanity. If NBIC convergence is limited to the observation of integrating four scientific disciplines, CKTS in contrast takes a resolutely solutionist position, similar to transhumanist-singularist thought.

It should be noted that, in 2013, the European Commission supported all projects promoting the convergence of nanotechnology, nano-biology and healthcare domains, positioning itself in a dynamic compatible with that of CKTS. When we speak of the economy of knowledge model, this relies on the dynamic of CKTS, which uses knowledge and technology as vectors for growth [ROC 03].

In its definition, the concept of CKTS sides with technoprogressism, which does not envisage the eventuality of using knowledge and technology without immediate benefit for society or to the benefit of only a fraction of society. Technologically conservative thought does not share the underlying optimism conveyed by CKTS. Genetic manipulation, gene editing and artificial intelligence incite debate with the sometimes entrenched positions of those who see these disciplines only as threats to society and the human species.

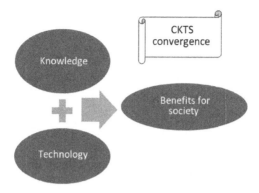

Figure 7.2. *CKTS*

7.5. Convergence M-I (Material-Information)

This material-information convergence comes from an approach resulting from theoretical physics and the feedback loops that operate between the physical space and the data space. It establishes the evolutionary link between the material, which can encode the information, and this information, which is becoming ubiquitous in physical space. Concretely, this research is carried out to make calculations at the atomic level and to create memory spaces on this scale. Man's contribution to M-I convergence is watermarked while remaining present, since it is mankind that still supervises the calculating power and information storage. We note that the concept of M-I convergence goes against entropic evolution (second principle) without contradicting this thermodynamic law.

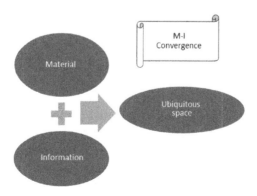

Figure 7.3. *M-I convergence*

7.6. The spread of artificial intelligence to domains of human expertise

In 2016, artificial intelligence surpassed human beings in several domains hitherto reserved for human ability alone. This deep-rooted trend is accelerating without it being possible to evaluate precisely what AI could come to govern between now and 2025. The number of wins by AI in 2016, in competition between mankind and machines, gives rise to questions, fears and nightmares among supporters and detractors of AI. It has been shown that all sectors of human activity are affected by this transfer of expertise.

Thus, in 2016, Smart Tissue Autonomous Robot (STAR), the surgeon robot, succeeded in operating on pig intestines autonomously with a remarkable quality of surgical intervention. A platform developed by Microsoft in collaboration with ING Bank and Delft University of Technology created, via a 3D impression, a human portrait in the style of Rembrandt with extraordinary intensity following a machine learning process using all the master's works.

The AlphaGo (DeepMind Google) artificial intelligence outwitted the world champion of the game *Go*, Lee Sedol, beating him four times. A second AI named Libratus, developed by a team of researchers at the American Carnegie Mellon University, was shown playing poker, beating four professional players during a tournament (January 2017). Finally, we expect DeepMind Google to develop an AI that can lip-read with a success rate of 46.8%, while the best human experts could not achieve a success rate of over 15%.

These examples where AI has the advantage multiplied in 2016 include activities linked to human resources in business with, for example, intelligent CV analysts, which were able to categorize large volumes of CVs while keeping them pertinent to the ranking of applications.

Prospective studies carried out by large American consulting firms have put forward various, sometimes debatable, figures on the percentage of professions and competencies to be transferred to AI to the detriment of human skills. It is certainly impossible to predict the speed with which domains of human expertise will be transferred to artificial intelligence and the extent of its spread by 2025.

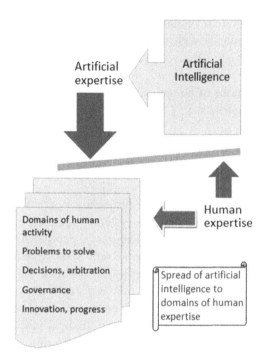

Figure 7.4. *Mechanism of the spread of artificial intelligence to domains of human expertise*

The impact of the spread of artificial intelligence to domains of human expertise will be global, not sparing any sector. The economic effects are beginning to make themselves felt with, for example, the replacement of entire teams of engineers in Japan in the domain of insurance (risk calculation) by intelligent platforms such as IBM Watson.

Industrial production was the first to use the power of artificial intelligence by replacing human operators with robotic units. Medicine in general and some of its specialisms such as radiology will soon undergo the same disruption with a rapid spread of artificial intelligence to domains of human expertise, which will oblige doctors to reposition their practice, in contact with powerful systems producing diagnostics and predictive analyses. Legal experts, lawyers, solicitors and magistrates will integrate and use contributions from artificial intelligence, as well as teachers, decision-makers and civil and military strategists.

The education system should already be seeking to educate pupils with a view to complementarity with what AI will be able to govern. Without this adaptation in the acquisition of knowledge and competencies, the aim of CKTS will not be reached and the effects of the spread of artificial intelligence to domains of human expertise will, on the contrary, be counter-productive and destructive. These subtle balances must be invented by mankind and its AI.

7.7. Global algorithmic projection and technology convergences

The formalism of the algorithmic projection P_S (H/A) of an individual H according to an algorithm A run on a system S does not presuppose anything about the system itself, its location, features or perimeter. On the contrary, it distinguishes the human user H of the system S, on which the algorithm A is run, without taking account of the physical distance separating the system from the individual. Indeed, NBIC convergence makes this distance tend toward zero with the appearance of connected implants and prostheses endowed with calculating capacity. Future medical neuro-implants used in treating diseases of the brain will possess calculating power and produce algorithmic projections inside the human body. The interfacing between the brain and the neuromorphic connections will trigger a hybridization, followed by a fusion of H and S under the effect of NBIC convergence.

In civil and military domains, the concepts of human augmentation and the augmented individual will be applied to global algorithmic projections. They will participate in augmenting the individual as a vector for augmentation, as well as themselves be subject to digital augmentations.

An individual's global algorithmic projection will benefit from all the progress in artificial intelligence by gaining in structure and dynamic organization. In the medium term, it should be imagined as a body of information endowed with a "digital central nervous system" responsible for creating a hierarchy of data in real time and structuring it while faithfully reflecting (without a loss of information) the individual's lived experience.

The global algorithmic projection, avatar, digital double or projective reflection should thus gain in dynamism and then come alive thanks to artificial intelligence.

Henceforth, extremely profound questions will be asked, concerning our free will and evolution:

– How will we interact with our own global algorithmic projections?

– What influence will they have on us, our thoughts, our actions?

– What degree of autonomy will they have?

– In what forms will they interact with one another?

– Will they all be interconnected so as to only create a single and unique universal global projection, or a digital reflection as a whole?

– If so, how will this universal algorithmic projection accommodate the entropy principle?

Of course, the answers to the above six questions are left to the readers' imagination and to that of their global algorithmic projection.

Appendix

Translations of the fake message used after the Vinci HoaxCrash

New VINCI Press release

Rueil Malmaison, 22nd November 2016

Vinci is launching a review of accounts consolidated for the year 2015 and the first half of 2016

Vinci today announced its intention to review those of its accounts consolidated for the 2015 fiscal year as well as for the first half of 2016. The results of an internal audit by the Vinci group have in fact revealed that irregular transfers of the group's operating expenses were made to its balance sheet, in breach of all recognised accounting principles. The total of these transfers rose to 2490 million euros for the 2015 fiscal year and 1065 million euros for the first half of 2016. According to the internal audit, real, operational results were 1225 million for 2015 and 641 million for the first half of 2016. The group therefore reported a net loss for 2015 as well as for the first half of 2016.

Vinci quickly informed its external auditors (KPMG and Deloitte and Associates) of the discovery of these transfers. On 21st November, KPMG informed Vinci that in light of these irregularities, its audit of accounts consolidated in 2015 and the first half of 2016 would not be valid.

Vinci will publish its unaudited accounts for the 2015 fiscal year as well as for the first half of 2016 as soon as possible. Once a new audit has been achieved, Vinci will publish new audited accounts for both periods. The group has moreover launched a full review of its internal regulations in its financial management.

The company has dismissed Christian Labeyrie, Vinci's joint general director and financial director.

Vinci has informed the Financial Markets Authority (FMA) of these events.

The review of operational results for 2015 and 2016 should have no consequences for the groups finances and should not affect the group's clients or financial obligations.

"Our management team is very shocked by these discoveries", said Xavier Huillard, Vinci's Chairman and CEO. "We are committed to ensuring that Vinci meets the highest ethical standards in conducting the group's business".

"Our clients as well as our employees should continue to have confidence in the Vinci group's viability and its long-term engagement. In no instance has our service been affected by these events and our committment to meeting our customers' needs remains a priority. The rumours circulating of insolvency proceedings are entirely false", added Vinci's Chairman and CEO. "We are committed to implementing the necessary changes within the group".

The Vinci group will hold a press conference tomorrow.

Media Contact
Paul-Alexis Bouquet
Tel: +33 (0)751 93 47 48

Bibliography

[AGE 09] AGENCE D'URBANISME POUR LE DÉVELOPPEMENT DE L'AGGLOMÉRATION LYONNAISE, *Proceedings of Villes & Numérique, nouveaux usages, nouveaux visages*, July 2009.

[ARQ 93] ARQUILLA J., RONFELDT D., "Cyberwar is Coming!", *Comparative Strategy*, vol. 12, no. 2, pp. 141–165, 1993.

[AUR 94] AUROUX S., *La révolution technologique de la grammatisation*, Mardaga, Liège, 1994.

[BAB 15] BABINET G., VASSOYAN R. (eds), Big data et objets connectés, Report, Institut Montaigne, April 2015.

[BAC 99] BACHIMONT B., "De l'hypertexte à l'hypotexte : les parcours de la mémoire documentaire", in LENAY C., HAVELANGE V. (eds), *Mémoire de la technique et techniques de la mémoire*, Érès, Toulouse, 1999.

[BAC 00a] BACHIMONT B., "Engagement sémantique et engagement ontologique : conception et réalisation d'ontologies en Ingénierie des connaissances", in CHARLES J., ZACKLAND M., KASSEL G. *et al.* (eds), *Ingénierie des connaissances, évolutions récentes et nouveaux défis*, Eyrolles, Paris, 2000.

[BAC 00b] BACHIMONT B., "L'intelligence artificielle comme écriture dynamique : de la raison graphique à la raison computationnelle", in PETIOT J., FABBRI P. (eds), *Au nom du sens*, Grasset, Paris, available at: http://www.utc.fr/~bachimon/Publications_attachments/BachimontCerisy1996.pdf, 2000.

[BAC 04a] BACHIMONT B., Arts et Sciences du numérique : ingénierie des connaissances et critique de la raison, PhD thesis, UTC, Compiègne, available at: http://www.utc.fr/~bachimon/Livresettheses_attachments/HabilitationBB.pdf, 2004.

[BAC 04b] BACHIMONT B., "Signes formels et computation numérique : entre intuition et formalisme", in SCHRAMM H., SCHWARTE L., LAZARDZIG J. (eds), *Instrumente in Kunst Und Wissenschaft*, Walter de Gruyter Verlag, Berlin, 2004.

[BAC 10] BACHIMONT B., *Le sens de la technique : Le numérique et le calcul*, Les Belles Lettres, Paris, 2010.

[BAC 12] BACHIMONT B., "Pour une critique phénoménologique de la raison computationnelle", in FRAU-MEIGS D., BRUILLARD É., DELAMOTTE É. (eds), *E-dossier de l'audiovisuel : L'éducation aux cultures de l'information*, available at: http://www.ina-expert.com/e-dossier-de-l-audiovisuel-l-education-aux-cultures-de-l-information/pour-une-critique-phenomenologique-de-la-raison-computationnelle.html, 2012.

[BAR 57] BARTHES R., *Mythologies*, Le Seuil, Paris, 1957.

[BAR 80] BARTHES R., *La chambre claire : Note sur la photographie*, Le Seuil, Paris, 1980.

[BEI 13] BEIJAFLORE CABINET, Cyber sûreté & Cyber sécurité, BC Report, November 2013.

[BER 13a] BERTHIER T., "Projections algorithmiques et cyberespace", *Revue internationale d'intelligence économique*, vol. 5, no. 2, pp. 179–195, 2013.

[BER 13b] BERTHIER T., "Concurrences et duels algorithmiques", *Revue de Défense Nationale*, vol. 761, 2013.

[BER 13c] BERTHIER T., "Créons l'observatoire des évolutions algorithmiques", *Défense et Sécurité Internationale*, May 2013.

[BER 14a] BERTHIER T., "Sur la valeur d'une donnée", *Publications de la Chaire de cyberdéfense Saint-Cyr-Sogeti-Thales*, May 2014.

[BER 14b] BERTHIER T., "Newscaster, l'opération iranienne", *Vérification sur Internet : quand les réseaux doutent de tout*, Observatoire géostratégique de l'information, IRIS, pp. 12–14, November 2014.

[BER 14c] BERTHIER T., *Cyberchronique – Décomposition systémique d'une cyberattaque, dissymétries et antifragilité*, Publications de la chaire de cyberstratégie CASTEX, January 2014.

[BER 15a] BERTHIER T., BRUNO B., "Les structures de données fictives utilisées en ingénierie sociale", *Revue de la Gendarmerie Nationale*, 4th quarter, 2015.

[BER 15b] BERTHIER T., KEMPF O., "Ville connectée et algorithmes prédictifs", *Digital Polis Conference Proceedings*, Paris, 2015.

[BER 15c] BERTHIER T., TEBOUL B., "Valeur et Véracité de la donnée : enjeux pour l'entreprise et défis pour le Data Scientiste", *La donnée n'est pas donnée Conference Proceedings*, Ecole Militaire, 23 March 2015.

[BIR 09] BIRD S., KLEIN E., LOPE E., *Natural Language Processing with Python*, O'Reilly Media, Farnham, 2009.

[BOY 12] BOYER B., *Cyberstratégie, l'art de la guerre numérique*, Nuvis, Paris, 2012.

[BUL 13] BULUSU L., *Open Source, Data Warehousing and Business Intelligence*, CRC Press, Boca Raton, 2013.

[CAR 10] CARNAP R., "Manifeste du Cercle de Vienne", in SOULEZ A. (ed.), *Le dépassement de la métaphysique par l'analyse logique du langage*, Vrin, Paris, 2010.

[CAR 12] CARDON D., "Regarder les données", *Multitudes*, vol. 33, no. 49, pp. 138–142, available at: http://www.multitudes.net/regarder-les-donnees/, 2012.

[CAR 13a] CARDON D., "Du lien au like sur internet, Deux mesures de la réputation", *Communications*, no. 93, pp. 173–186, 2013.

[CAR 13b] CARDON D., "Dans l'esprit du PageRank, Une enquête sur l'algorithme de Google", *Réseaux*, no. 177, pp. 63–95, 2013.

[CAR 15] CARDON D., *A quoi rêvent les algorithmes, La République des Idées*, Le Seuil, Paris, 2015.

[CHA 08] CHAZAUD N., Réputation d'entreprise et veille informationnelle : vers un modèle anticipatif de gestion des risques de réputation sur internet, PhD thesis, University of Montpellier, 2008.

[CHU 01] CHUN R., DAVIES G., "E-Reputation and the Role of Mission and Vision Statements", *Journal of Brand Management*, vol. 8, no. 4, 2001.

[CIG 14] CIGREF, Enjeux business des données : Comment gérer les données de l'entreprise pour créer de la valeur ?, Report, 2014.

[COL 14] COLLINS, *Collins English Dictionary*, Harper Collins, London, 2014.

[CUR 16] CURBATOV P., LOUYOT-GALLICHER M., "Convergence NBIC et Knowledge Marketing", *International Marketing Trends Conference*, Venice, available at: https://hal.archives-ouvertes.fr/hal-01364860/document, 2016.

[DAN 13] DANIELOU J., MENARD F., L'art d'augmenter les villes, (pour) une enquête sur la ville intelligente, PUCA report, September 2013.

[DAT 15] DATTA A. et al., "Automated Experiments on Ad Privacy Settings: A Tale of Opacity, Choice, and Discrimination", *PoPETs*, no. 1, pp. 92–112, available at: http://www.degruyter.com/view/j/popets.2015.1.issue-1/popets-2015- 0007/popets-2015-0007.xml, 2015.

[DEL 90] DELEUZE G., *Pourparlers*, Les Editions de Minuit, Paris, 1990.

[DER 64] DERRIDA J., "Violence et métaphysique. Essai sur la pensée d'Emmanuel Lévinas", *Revue de Métaphysique et de Morale*, pp. 425–473, 1964.

[DER 67a] DERRIDA J., *De la grammatologie*, Les Editions de Minuit, Paris, 1967.

[DER 67b] DERRIDA J., *L'Écriture et la différence*, Le Seuil, Paris, 1967.

[DER 71] DERRIDA J., "Signature, événement, context", *Congrès international des Sociétés de philosophie de langue française*, Montreal, 1971.

[DER 72a] DERRIDA J., *Marges de la philosophie*, Les Éditions de Minuit, 1972.

[DER 72b] DERRIDA J., *La dissémination*, Le Seuil, Paris, 1972.

[DER 75] DE ROSNAY J., *Le macroscope : vers une vision globale*, Le Seuil, Paris, 1975.

[DGC 13] DG CONNECT, A European strategy on the data value chain, Report, European Commission, 2013.

[DOM 10] DOMOTIQUE NEWS, Ville numérique U-Songdo, Report no. 248, September 2010.

[DOS 11] DOSSÉ S., KEMPF O. (eds), *Stratégies dans le cyberspace*, L'esprit du livre, Sceaux, 2011.

[DOS 13] DOSSÉ S., KEMPF O., MALIS C., *Le cyberspace, Nouveau domaine de la pensée stratégique*, Economica, Paris, 2013.

[DUL 17] DULONG DE ROSNAY M., "Les traces de l'activité humaine dans le numérique", in BOUZEGHOUB M., MOSSERY R. (eds), *Les Big Data à Découvert*, CNRS Editions, Paris, 2017.

[EVE 14] EVENO E., MESTRES J.M., "Villes numériques, villes intelligentes ?", *Revue Urbanisme*, no. 384, pp. 24–84, 2014.

[FEL 13] FELSTINER A., "The weakness of crowds", *Crowds and Clouds*, no. 2, 2013.

[GAL 10] GALE INTERNATIONAL, City Builder – Songdo, Report, 2010.

[GAL 13] GALINON-MELENEC B., ZLITNI S., *L'Homme-trace, producteur de traces numériques*, CNRS Editions, Paris, 2013.

[GEO 09] GEORGES F., "Identité numérique et représentation de soi", *Réseaux*, vol. 154, pp.165–193, 2009.

[GHI 12] GHITALLA F., "Converser avec les données numériques", *L'atelier de cartographie*, available at: https://ateliercartographie.files.wordpress.com/2011/04/postdatav2.pdf, 2012.

[GIN 89] GINZBURG C., *Mythes, emblèmes, traces*, Flammarion, Paris, 1989.

[GLA 15] GLASSEY O., "Des communautés virtuelles aux big data : les formes sociales des promesses des technologies de l'information", in AUDÉTAT M. (ed.), *Sciences et technologies émergentes : pourquoi tant de promesses ?*, Editions Hermann, Paris, 2015.

[GOO 79] GOODY J., *La raison graphique : la domestication de la pensée sauvage*, Les Editions de Minuit, Paris, 1979.

[GRE 03] GREISCH J., "Trace et oubli : entre la menace de l'effacement et l'insistance de l'ineffaçable", *Diogène*, no. 201, pp. 82–106, 2003.

[GUC 10] GUCHET X., *Pour un humanisme technologique : Culture technique et société dans la philosophie de Gilbert Simondon*, PUF, Paris, 2010.

[HAG 17] HAGER S., LENOIR E., De la cybercriminalité à la fraude : une menace en pleine mutation, Report, Euler Hermes, DFCG, May 2017.

[HAR 90] HARAWAY D., *Simians, Cyborgs and Women : The Reinvention of Nature*, Routledge, London, 1990.

[HEI 54] HEIDEGGER M., *La question de la technique : Essais et conferences*, Gallimard, Paris, 1954.

[HEI 87] HEIDEGGER M., *Chemins qui ne mènent nulle part*, Gallimard, Paris, 1987.

[HIG 10] HIGH LEVEL EXPERT GROUP ON SCIENTIFIC DATA, Riding the Wave: How Europe can gain from the rising tide of scientific data, Report, European Commission, 2010.

[IBM 11] IBM, Vestas: Turning climate into capital with Big Data, Report, 2011.

[IBM 12a] IBM, A collection of Big Data client success stories, Report, 2012.

[IBM 12b] IBM, The Case for Business Analytics in Midsize Firms – Cincinnati Zoo, Report, 2012.

[IFR 10] IFRAH L., *L'information et le renseignement par internet*, Paris, PUF, 2010.

[JAC 15] JACOBS B., Écritures algorithmiques, Incursion aux confins de la poétique computationnelle de mise en donnée des traces numériques, Lecture notes, UTC, Compiègne, 2015.

[JAN 11a] JANERT P.K., *Data Analysis with Open Source Tools*, O'Reilly Media, Farnham, 2011.

[JEA 11b] JEANNERET Y., "Complexité de la notion de trace, De la traque au trace", in GALINON-MÉLÉNEC B. (ed.), *L'homme trace*, CNRS Editions, Paris, 2011.

[KEM 12] KEMPF O., *Introduction à la cyberstratégie*, Economica, Paris, 2012.

[KEM 14] KEMPF O., BERTHIER T., "L'armée syrienne électronique : entre cyberagression et guerre de l'information", *Revue de la Défense Nationale – "Guerre de l'information"*, May 2014.

[KRÄ 07] KRÄMER S., "Qu'est-ce donc qu'une trace, et quelle est sa fonction épistémologique ? État des lieux", in KRÄMER S., KOGGE W., GRUBE G. (eds), *Spur: Spurenlesen als Orientierungstechnik und Wissenskunst*, Suhrkamp, Frankfurt, 2007.

[LAT 13] LATOUR B., "Facing Gaia: Six lectures on the Political Theology of Nature", *Gifford Lectures in Natural Theology*, Edinburgh, February 2013.

[LEE 13] LEE Y.W., Ubiquitous (smart) City, EU Parliament Seminar, April 2013.

[LES 76] LESOURNE J., *Les systèmes du destin*, Dalloz, Paris, 1976.

[LEV 74a] LEVINAS E., *Autrement qu'être ou au-delà de l'essence*, M. Nijhoff, The Hague, 1974.

[LEV 74b] LEVINAS E., *En découvrant l'existence avec Husserl et Heidegger*, Vrin, Paris, 1974.

[LEV 98] LEVINAS E., *De Dieu qui vient à l'idée*, Vrin, Paris, 1998.

[MCD 02] MCDONALD C.G., SLAWSON V.C., "Reputation in an Internet Auction Market", *Economic Inquiry*, vol. 40, no. 3, pp. 633–650, 2002.

[MCK 11] MCKINSEY GLOBAL INSTITUTE, Big Data: The next frontier for innovation, competition, and productivity, Report, May 2011.

[MER 09a] MERZEAU L., "Du signe à la trace", in BOUGNOUX D. (ed.), *Empreintes de Roland Barthes*, Éditions Cécile Defaut, Nantes, available at: https://halshs.archives-ouvertes.fr/halshs-00483302/document, 2009.

[MER 09b] MERZEAU L., "Du signe à la trace : l'information sur mesure", *Hermès, La Revue*, no. 53, pp. 23–29, available at: https://halshs.archives-ouvertes.fr/halshs-00483292/document, 2009.

[MER 09c] MERZEAU L., "Présence numérique : les médiations de l'identité", *Les Enjeux de l'Information et de la Communication*, vol. 2009, no. 1, available at: http://lesenjeux.u-grenoble3.fr/2009/Merzeau/index.php, 2009.

[MER 09d] MERZEAU L., "Présence numérique : du symbolique à la trace", *Médiation et information*, no. 29, pp. 153–163, available at: https://halshs.archives-ouvertes.fr/halshs-00487255/document, 2009.

[MER 13] MERZEAU L., "L'intelligence des traces", *Intellectica*, vol. 1, no. 59, pp. 115–135, available at: https://halshs.archives-ouvertes.fr/halshs-01071211/document, 2013.

[MES 13] MESSIAS J., SCHMIDT L., OLIVIERA R. *et al.*, "You followed my bot! Transforming robots into influential users in Twitter", *First Monday*, vol. 18, no. 7, 2013.

[MIL 13] MILLE A., "Des traces à l'ère du Web", *Intellectica*, vol. 1, no. 59, pp. 7–28, 2013.

[OSO 18] OSoME, BotOrNot, available at: http://truthy.indiana.edu/botornot/, 2018.

[PAR 11] PARISER E., *The Filter Bubble: What the Internet is Hiding from You*, Penguin Press, New York, 2011.

[PAT 12] PATIL D.J., "Data Jujitsu: The Art of Turning Data into Product", *Strata Conference*, Santa Clara, available at: http://strataconf.com/strata2012/public/schedule/detail/23092, March 2012.

[PED 06] PEDAUQUE T., *Le document à la lumière du numérique*, C&F Éditions, Caen, 2006.

[PEI 84] PEIRCE C.S., *Textes anticartésiens*, Aubier, Paris, 1984.

[PEI 89] PEIRCE C.S., *Collected Papers*, vol. 8, Harvard University Press, Cambridge, 1989.

[PEI 03] PEIRCE C.S., *Pragmatisme et Sciences Normatives*, Éditions du Cerf, Paris, 2003.

[PEI 06] PEIRCE C.S., *Écrits Logiques*, Éditions du Cerf, Paris, 2006.

[PER 89] PEREC G., *L'infra-ordinaire*, Le Seuil, Paris, 1989.

[RIC 00] RICOEUR P., *La mémoire l'histoire, l'oubli*, Le Seuil, Paris, 2000.

[RIE 10] RIEDER B., "Pratiques informationnelles et analyse des traces numériques : de la représentation à l'intervention", *Études de communication*, no. 35, available at: http://edc.revues.org/2249, 2010.

[ROC 03] ROCO M.C., BAINBRIDGE W.S. (eds), Converging Technologies for Improving Human Performance, Report, NSF/DOC, available at: http://www. wtec.org/ConvergingTechnologies/Report/NBIC_report.pdf, 2003.

[ROC 13] ROCO M.C., BAINBRIDGE W.S., TONN B. *et al.*, Convergence of Knowledge, Technology, and Society: Beyond Convergence of Nano-Bio-Info-Cognitive Technologies, Report, World Technology Evaluation Center, available at: http://www.wtec.org/NBIC2/Docs/WTEC-Convergence%20of%20KTS-0108 14.pdf, 2013.

[ROS 17] DE ROSNAY M., "Les traces de l'activité humaine dans le numérique", in MOKRANE B., RÉMY M. (eds), *Les Big Data à Découvert*, CNRS Editions, Paris, 2017.

[ROU 10] ROUVROY A., BERNS T., "Le nouveau pouvoir statistique", *Multitudes*, no. 40, pp. 88–103, available at: http://www.cairn.info/revue-multitudes-2010-1-page-88.htm, 2010.

[ROU 12] ROUVROY A., "The end(s) of critique: data-behaviorism vs. due-process", in DE VRIES K., HILDEBRANDT M. (eds), *Privacy, Due Process and the Computational Turn*, available at: http://works.bepress.com/antoinette_rouvroy/ 44/, 2012.

[ROU 13] ROUVROY A., BERNS T., "Gouvernementalité algorithmique et perspectives d'émancipation. Le disparate comme condition d'individuation par la relation ?", *Réseaux*, no. 177, pp. 163–196, available at: http://www.cairn. info/resume.php?ID_ARTICLE=RES_177_0163, 2013.

[ROU 15a] ROUVROY A., "Big data is algorithming you", *Article11*, no. 17, available at: http://www.article11.info/?Big-Data-is-algorithming-you, 2015.

[ROU 15b] ROUVROY A., "L'algorithme n'est pas un système de prédiction mais d'intervention", *Médiapart*, interview with Jérôme Hourdeaux, available at: http://www.mediapart.fr/journal/france/250515/lalgorithme-nest-pas-un-systeme-de-prediction-mais-d-intervention, 2015.

[RYA 10] RYAN T., Getting in Bed with Robin Sage, Blackhat Briefings and Training, available at: https://www.privacywonk.net/download/BlackHat-USA-2010-Ryan-Getting-In-Bed-With-Robin-Sage-v1.0.pdf, 2010.

[SER 02] SERRES A., Quelle(s) problématique(s) de la trace ?, CERCOR seminar, 2002.

[SIM 58] SIMONDON G., *Du mode d'existence des objets techniques*, Aubier, Paris, 1958.

[SIN 08] SINGHAL A., Introduction to Google Ranking, Google Official Blog, available at: https://sites.google.com/site/webmasterhelpforum/informations-supplementaires- concernant-la-creation-de-sites-de-qualite, July 2008.

[SLO 00] SLOTERDIJK P., *La domestication de l'Être : Pour un éclaircissement de la clairière*, Mille et une nuits, Paris, 2000.

[SOU 85] SOULEZ A., *Manifeste du Cercle de Vienne et autres écrits*, PUF, Paris, 1985.

[STE 10] STEINER P., "Philosophie, technologie et cognition", *Intellectica*, vols 1–2, no. 53/54, pp. 7–40, 2010.

[STI 94] STIEGLER B., *La technique et le temps 1 : La faute d'Épiméthée*, Galilée, Paris, 1994.

[STI 96] STIEGLER B., *La technique et le temps 2 : La désorientation*, Galilée, Paris, 1996.

[TAL 07] TALEB N.N., *The Black Swan: The Impact of the Highly Improbable*, Random House, New York, 2007.

[TAL 12] TALEB N.N., *Antifragile: Things That Gain From Disorder*, Random House, New York, 2012.

[TEB 14] TEBOUL B., AMRI T., "Les Machines pour le Big Data : Vers une Informatique Quantique et Cognitive", Preprint, 2014.

[TEB 16] TEBOUL B., Le développement du neuromarketing aux États-Unis et en France : Acteurs-réseaux, traces et controverses, PhD thesis, PSL Research University, September 2016.

[TEB 17] TEBOUL B., *Robotariat : Critique de l'automatisation de la société*, Editions Kawa, Paris, 2017.

[TEC 14] TECHNOLOGY REVIEW, Bot Detection, available at: http://www.technologyreview.com/529461/how-to-spot-a-social-bot-on-twitter, 2014.

[TIE 13] TIERCELIN C., *Peirce et le pragmatisme*, PUF, Paris, 2013.

[TUR 36] TURING A., "On Computable numbers, with an application to the entscheidungsproblem", *Proceedings of the London Mathematical Society*, vol. 42/2, pp. 230–265, available at: https://www.cs.virginia.edu/~robins/Turing_Paper_1936.pdf, 1936.

[TUR 46] TURING A., "Proposal for Development in the Mathematics Division of an Automatic Computing Engine (ACE)", in CARPENTER B.E., DORAN R.W. (eds), *A.M Turing's ACE report of 1946 and other papers*, MIT Press, Cambridge, 1946.

[TUR 50] TURING A., "Computing machinery and intelligence", *Mind*, no. 59, pp. 433–460, available at: http://www.loebner.net/Prizef/TuringArticle.html, 1950.

[VAN 99] VANDENDORP C., *Du Papyrus à l'Hypertexte : Essai sur les mutations du livre et de la lecture*, La Découverte, Paris, 1999.

[VAN 16] VAN ESTE R., STEMERDING D., RERIMASSIE V. *et al.*, De BIO à la convergence NBIC, Report, Council of Europe, available at: https://rm. coe.int/CoERMPublicCommonSearchServices/DisplayDCTMContent?document Id=0900001680307576, 2016.

[VEN 09] VENTRE D., *Information Warfare*, ISTE Ltd, London and John Wiley & Sons, New York, 2009.

[VEN 11] VENTRE D. (ed.), *Cyberwar and Information Warfare*, ISTE Ltd, London and John Wiley & Sons, New York, 2011.

[VON 45] VON NEUMANN J., "First draft of a report on the EDVAC", *IEEE Annals of the History of Computing*, vol. 15/4, no. 1993, pp. 27–75, 1945.

[ZEN 16] ZENETTI M.J., "Spectres photographiques : quand la photographie hante la littérature", *Conserveries mémorielles*, no. 18, available at: http://journals. openedition.org/cm/2281, 2016.

Index

A, B, C

anonymity, 85, 87
archived, 27–29, 31, 36, 37, 44, 48
artificial intelligence, 129, 139, 141,
    142, 144–146
    spread of to domains of human
        expertise, 140, 144–146
BEC, 118, 119, 129–132, 135
big data, 69, 71, 75, 79–83
biotechnologies, 139–142
CKTS, 140, 142, 143, 146
cognitive science, 139–142
competition, 37, 39, 43, 47
confidence, 114, 115, 117, 131
convergence
    M-I, 143
    NBIC, 139–142, 146
    technological, 139
critical, 1, 15, 16
cyber-espionage, 113, 114
cybernetics, 20
cybersecurity, 87, 98, 99, 104–107

D, E, F

Derrida, 1, 11–16, 19
detection, 119, 130, 135–138
digital reflection, 24, 33

disinformation, 94
duels, 43, 44, 47
e-reputation, 31, 39–43
Facebook, 87–93, 96, 99, 100, 107,
    108, 110
fake profile, 85, 87–89, 91–94, 97,
    98, 105
false transfer orders, 118, 119, 129,
    130, 134, 135
feedback loops, 63, 64, 66
fictitious
    data, 85, 87, 100, 104, 105,
        108, 112
    structures, 119, 137, 138
    projection, 100, 102, 103

G, H, I

global projection, 33, 34, 47, 48
Heidegger, 1, 6, 11, 12, 15
HoaxCrash, 118–120, 122–124,
    127–129, 135–138
identity, 19, 87, 89, 97, 100, 101,
    102, 105, 106
imprint, 1–6, 12, 18, 19, 22
index, 5, 8
influence, 90, 93–96, 110, 111,
    118, 123, 136

intelligent city, 58, 60, 61, 66
interaction, 23, 24, 26, 32, 33, 39,
    40, 44, 47

L, M, N, P

Lévinas, 1, 11, 14–16
logical, 5, 8, 22
metadata, 24, 27, 28, 36–38
nanotechnology, 139–142
philosophy, 1
popularity, 89, 90
predictive
    algorithmic infrastructure, 66
    algorithms, 63–66

Q, R, S

quality, 80
random, 63–66
retrieval, 67, 68, 71

sign, 1, 5, 8–11, 13, 15, 22
social
    bots, 93–96
    networks, 87–93, 96, 97, 99, 102,
        103, 105, 106, 108, 110, 111
S-projection, 24, 31–33, 35, 44, 47
systemic, 23–25, 29, 30, 33, 34, 36,
    39–44, 47, 49, 55–59, 63–66

T, U, V

theft, 87, 89, 97, 100–102, 106
Twitter, 89–96, 99
ubiquitous city, 56, 58–63, 66
U-Songdo, 56, 60, 62, 63
value
    impact, 68, 69, 71, 72, 76, 77,
        79, 84
    instantaneous, 68, 69, 72, 73,
        75–79
    interpretation, 74, 77, 79
veracity, 89, 104

Printed in the United States
By Bookmasters